To Jep & Joyce

with thanks for your
inspiration and encouragement

love,

Fear or Freedom?

Fear or Freedom?

Why a warring church must change

Edited by

Simon Barrow

Shoving Leopard / Ekklesia

First published in 2008 by

Shoving Leopard
Flat 2F3, 8 Edina Street
Edinburgh
EH7 5PN
United Kingdom
http://www.shovingleopard.com/

Ekklesia
2nd Floor, 145-157 St John Street
London
EC1V 4PY
United Kingdom
http://ekklesia.co.uk/

ISBN 978 1 905565 14 6

Contents

Acknowledgements

The editor would like to extend a large 'thank you' to all who have contributed essays to this book, and especially to Savi Hensman, whose contributions to the work of Ekklesia and other networks of social change are very highly valued. Specific acknowledgments for re-use of material are noted at the end of the individual chapters.

It has been a great pleasure to renew my working relationship and friendship with the wonderful Janet de Vigne of Shoving Leopard. She's amazing. Thanks also to Nial Smith for his cover.

I am especially glad to be publishing some excerpts from the valuable work of Professor Deirdre Good. We had hoped that a UK edition of her book *Jesus' Family Values* (Church Publishing, 2007, USA), which in my view should be required reading for everyone at Lambeth 2008, would be possible. Unfortunately, due to the whims of publishing, it was not so. At least, not yet. This is a small compensation, I hope. Deirdre and I have deep family connections going back over 50 years, but we have only got to know each other personally over the past 18 months. I am more grateful than I can say for this, and for meeting Julian Sheffield.

My directorial colleague and friend Jonathan Bartley deserves a particular thank you. He is an abundant source of inspiration, encouragement and practical wisdom in a whole range of ways – and, above all else, he is a tremendously generous, resourceful and talented human being and fellow disciple. It's an honour to work with you, Jonathan.

A word of additional thanks to Jordan Tchilingirian, who came to work on an internship with Ekklesia in September 2006, after completing a degree in Social and Political Sciences at the University of Cambridge. His work on the wider significance of conflict in the Anglican Communion, particularly the Church of England, was invaluable in preparing this book.

Carla Roth, to whom I have the great privilege of being married, puts up with my inconveniences in all kinds of ways. This book is just one more, but not to be underestimated because of that.

This book is dedicated, in loving memory, to my parents, Belle and Leslie Padday-Barrow. My father, especially, bore the wounds that are spoken of in several places here in his body and deep in his soul.

Preface

I welcome this new collection of essays encouraging our churches to recover a vision of the Gospel of God's transforming love, shown to us in Jesus and offered for the whole world.

God's dream is that you and I and all of us will realise that we are family, that we are made for togetherness, for goodness, and for compassion.

In God's family, there are no outsiders, no enemies. Black and white, rich and poor, gay and straight – all belong. When we start to live as brothers and sisters and to recognise our interdependence, we become fully human.

Our world is facing many problems: poverty, HIV and AIDS (a devastating pandemic), environmental threat and war. God must be weeping looking at some of the atrocities that we commit against one another.

In the face of all of that, our church, especially the Anglican church at this time, is almost obsessed with questions of human sexuality. Yet there are so many issues crying out for concern and application by the church of its resources.

Our Communion has always been characterised by its comprehensiveness, its inclusiveness, and its catholicity. We are really family, held together not so much by law as by bonds of affection. There is no family that is unanimous on every single subject.

I beg all church members, in our Lord's name, agree to disagree, argue, debate, disagree, but do all this as members of one family.

We are most like God when we are welcoming and when we are as inclusive as possible, when we have broken down all middle walls of partition.

In a world where difference has led to alienation and even bloody conflict, the church is God's agent to demonstrate that unity in diversity is in fact the law of life.

Archbishop Emeritus Desmond Tutu
28 May 2008
Feast of St Augustine of Canterbury

Introduction: Fear or Freedom?

Pick up a newspaper, switch on the TV or log in to the Internet these days and it won't take you long to discover an argument involving religion. One of the most unpleasant, at least in terms of its overheated rhetoric and the personal acrimony it has occasioned, has been the long-running dispute within global Anglicanism – and many other Christian confessions, too – over sexuality, authority and the interpretation of the Bible. The row will gain more media attention at the Lambeth Conference of worldwide Anglican bishops in July 2008, though its final outcome is anyone's guess.

Many people not immediately caught up in this internecine conflict are intermittently baffled, bored and frustrated by it. What has such bitterness got to do with the Jesus of the gospels? Why is there so much fuss and attention directed towards a denomination that often appears a colonial hangover? What about the far more pressing issues of war, peace, development, environment, science and spirituality which people of faith and people of goodwill should be attending to? What on earth is Rowan Williams up to? And how does church infighting impact the credibility of the Christian message as a whole in the twenty-first century? These are some of the issues that concern us in these pages.

This collection of essays aims to probe behind and around these 'Anglican wars', not because this particular church deserves attention above others, but because the issues involved illustrate some important fault lines in Christianity as it enters an era which many of us in the West are calling, for want of a better term, 'post-Christendom'.

A church in turmoil and transition

The Church of England and its worldwide associates developed their ecclesial life out of a history shaped by the power of institutionalised religion. In the Europe of the Reformation and after, the church found its interests closely allied with the state. Its faith became a buttress to kings, princes and empires. It gave its blessing to the authorities in exchange for their protection and privilege. Establishment in England is a considerably attenuated and ameliorated version of this kind of settlement – miles away from Constantine's official sanction of Christianity in the Edict of Milan, but still founded on the idea of mutuality between those whose vocation is to direct "the life of the nation".

At the same time, however, and in a way that directly relates to the matters tackled in this book, Christianity in the West has been losing its control and influence dramatically over the past fifty years – the same period in which decolonisation, the end of the Cold war, the collapse of apartheid, the rise of globalisation and the growth of reactive forms of religion across the globe has been growing.

The result is a curious and unprecedented situation of change and insecurity for institutional faith, especially the inherited ecclesial structures and doctrines of the Christian churches. It is this dynamic, one that is still not widely understood, which lies behind all the arguments over ethics, control and interpretative power currently going on inside and beyond Anglicanism.

Meanwhile, it is the interweaving of Anglican fate, fortune and history with what has been happening on the world stage that makes its particular situation so interesting. The Christendom order is divided against itself, and the solutions or new possibilities that may emerge will require some major shifts in thinking and action if they are to be anything other than corrosive.

There is much to learn here for others: those from Catholic, Methodist, Baptist, Reformed, Lutheran, Anabaptist and dissenting perspectives; those reflecting from a greater spiritual distance on the role or impact of faith in today's world; those looking in from an interfaith or non-religious perspective. In different ways, Ekklesia, a UK-based think tank with a global network, seeks to address all those constituencies. Our agenda is to find ways of moving Christian thought beyond its usual pegs and pitfalls, and to reinstate the Gospel of radical emancipation (grace, peacemaking, restorative justice, hospitality, forgiveness and feasting) at the heart of the business of what it means to be church. This, we believe, is what is truly at stake in the disputes that could lead to what the media is insisting (rather inaccurately) in calling 'schism' within the Anglican Communion and elsewhere.

Beyond easy labels

Some years ago the interreligious theologian John Hick wrote of the emergence of 'two Christianities', one credally orthodox, conservative and authoritarian; the other free-floating, heterodox and flexible. This kind of division has hardened into something of a stereotype in today's media, where commentators often have little background in religion and its many crossbreeds.

We think the situation is more subtle and interesting than the generally accepted polarity allows. As Jonathan Bartley says in his chapter, post-Christendom Christianity is turning out to be more diverse than could ever have been imagined twenty years ago. If 'liberalism' involves abandoning the central tenets of Christianity for an allegedly better human ideology, then the people connected with the thinking going on around Ekklesia are not liberal, even though they most definitely cherish liberality.

Again, if 'conservative' means expecting solutions that require us to stick in a bygone world rather than engage with the present and the future, they are not conservative either, though they most certainly value ancient-new wisdom and believe there is something vital to be conserved and developed from the past.

The people who have contributed to this volume are also beyond easy 'party labels' beloved of those stoking church arguments, though that will not stop them being labelled – especially by people who do not like what they are saying. That's the way the game (the one we do not intend to play) goes. Most of these writers are Anglicans of one sort or another, though they also swim in larger seas, both ecclesially and in terms of their social engagement. Many have been actively supportive of Ekklesia's work, though none are in the least bound by it (other than, perhaps, the two directors!)

Not prescription, but regeneration

This book does not aim to give a comprehensive or systematic overview of what the churches are currently arguing about, or who is saying what. That kind of material is widely available elsewhere and will no doubt be flooding people's desktops and computers in the build up to, and aftermath of, Lambeth.

Our concern, rather, has been to collect together some essays which point towards the future church, the one tired of talking to itself; the one not over-preoccupied in trying to figure out ways that will keep it safe, secure, respectable and 'in control'. For the world is in a mess and there are far more important things to worry about, as Desmond Tutu makes plain.

Yet the church is of vital importance because, renewed in its vision of being a movement accompanying Jesus in the pains and joys of the world, rather than a fortress trying to preserve its own status, it can signal different habits, different possibilities, different options, and a different future which is the gift of God and does not 'belong' to any one of us in a proprietorial sense.

The overall tenor, therefore, aims to be hopeful as well as critical. There are five sections. The first looks at how Christian faith can be a source of inspiration and energy rather than a pool of anxiety and conflict. The second asks tough questions about what is going wrong, what virtues are needed instead, and why. The third looks at church, the family and the sexuality debate in the biblical, theological and ecumenical perspective. The fourth examines how we can learn from the Bible, from each other and from the traditions of thinking and conversing developed within the broad life of the Christian community. And the fifth addresses some horizons of change – our understanding of God, our sharing of the bread of life, and the invitation to move beyond a Christendom mentality.

Since a good deal of Ekklesia's work is in the areas of politics, public policy, social justice, peacemaking and human rights, the overtly 'theological' tone of much of the material in *Fear or Freedom?* may surprise some. But what we are aiming at in the first instance is not political prescription but spiritual regeneration, a change of heart, mind and purpose among the quarrelsome company of Christians.

These essays, many published before but substantially revised and re-ordered for the present volume, are seeking to give a flavour a of a different way of being church, for the sake of humanity and the world, rather than for an in-group or club. Nevertheless, they need to address the issues that arise within the Christian community, because these are matters that have a huge impact on society at large, and on the nature of the Gospel as it is developed, practised and proclaimed.

An overview of the book

For example, in her chapter carefully analysing the popular use and misuse of biblical and doctrinal language ('Being church in the freedom of God'), Savi Hensman shows that inflexible, one-sided, naïve or ideological conceptions of God in sections of the Christian tradition can reinforce domineering models and practices in the church – which is in fact supposed to be a creative vehicle of Jesus' broken body in the world, not a rigid institution.

God is not confined by rules set by humans and our structures, she argues, however powerful they may be by earthly standards. In the biblical tradition, God is at work outside as well as within institutions, including those that claim to be about God's business. Liberation, reformation and healing will continue to happen even if, at first, they are not acknowledged by the authorities (ecclesial and otherwise); and in time truth will break through our illusions.

This essay is highly relevant to issues being discussed in and beyond Anglicanism, concerning its disputed future, and in other sections of the worldwide Church. It may also give those beyond the church a better understanding of how language and tradition is being applied and misapplied within very diverse Christian communities during a time of considerable upheaval and anxiety.

Savi also writes tellingly about the use of scriptural precedent (alongside leading biblical scholars Chris Rowland and Deirdre Good), and about the development of reason and tradition specifically within Anglicanism. Deirdre's articles are drawn from her important book *Jesus' Family Values* (which has been published in the USA, but not so far on this side of the Atlantic) and from her contributions to Episcopal Café and Ekklesia, including a moving piece on the vocation of hospitality.

Other contributors include Anabaptist writer and peace activist Tim Nafziger, looking at the way anti-gay sentiment within conservative sections of the church has been alienating young people from the radical Evangelical tradition, and Anglican Catholic theologian and missiologist David Wood unpacking the meaning of down-to-earth faith ('the Word made flesh') for reformed Christian life and practice. Glynn Cardy, meanwhile, explores the models and metaphors of 'house' and 'ship' as ways of encouraging Christians to discover freedom and risk-taking.

My own articles include a re-examination of question of human sexuality from the perspective of ecumenism – by which I mean the shared work of Christians in the world, not ecclesiastical joinery. There is also a chapter about how Rowan Williams rightly continues to ruffle all parties in current Anglican disputes, another on what I might call 'the politics of Eucharistic living' and an opening piece on why a hope shaped by the example, death and risen life of Jesus can resource us to confront the crimes and misdemeanours of 'religion' and indeed much 'organised Christianity'.

The upshot of all this is not so much a conclusion as an invitation. As a troubled and troublesome bishop once put it, 'Even the church cannot keep a good God down'. More than that, Christians gathering and dispersing for the sake of a broken but glorious world can most surely learn to be a small part of the solution rather than a big part of the problem.

Simon Barrow
Ekklesia (www.ekklesia.co.uk)
Pentecost, 2008

Part One: Inspiring

Chapter One

How Christianity can kill or cure

Simon Barrow

It is hard to overestimate the divisions of the world right now. Even as the myth of unity-through-consumption is pumped out of our media monitors, the armies of one side confront the suicide bombers of another, each egged on by words of religious blessing.

Christians, to name but one segment of quarrelsome humanity, are split apart by violence, by wealth (or lack of it), by relations with those of other faiths and none, by arguments about sexuality, by politics, by culture, by the way they read the Bible, by authority claims, and by who and what they believe in.

When the events, resources and texts that are supposed to bring people together and proclaim healing merely reveal their apparent irreconcilability, is searching for commonality amidst radical religious difference a hopeless, abstract ideal? Can our divisions be healed? What hope conversation in place of cacophony?

As David Jenkins put it in his marvellous book, *The Contradiction of Christianity* (SCM Press, 1976), the fundamental issue is about "whether I am trapped in being me, whether every tribal 'we' is trapped in being an exclusive 'us' and whether there is any realistic hope of a way of being human which fulfils us all."

On the surface the evidence is clear. The behaviour of Christians and the performance of their institutions often render utterly incredible anything they might want to say about what the Gospel stands for. Christianity can cure, but equally it can kill.

Why bother with it, then? Well, the Christian conviction is that the Word of life has become flesh. This means that the 'answers' we seek are not to be found in infallible texts or unassailable propositions, but in and through the vulnerable humanity to which God is committed.

So the only response that is adequate both to the scale of our human dilemma and to the nature of what is unveiled in the Gospel is (quite against our instincts for tidiness and convenience) the difficult truth of a person.

A word of hope

In the counter-story and lived reality of Jesus of Nazareth – a narrative about being truly human, but also about a living God who is quite unlike our ideas of 'godness' – we see 'in the flesh' the surprising, redemptive potential of diversity in the face of division.

Put simply, Christ's is the less-travelled Way marked by open tables, acceptance of 'outsiders', refusal of violence, challenge to the rich, forgiveness and repentance, resistance to the powers-that-be, conflict through the cross, the foretaste of risen life, and the shock of the Spirit – the one who surprises us with liberated meaning.

What we long for in Jesus' company, therefore, is not mere 'tolerance' or illusory power for ourselves. It is the impossible possibility of God's domination-free kingdom (or 'kin-dom', as a South African theologian once beautifully put it).

The Gospel is about precisely this unimaginable love. It is a love that subjugates power so as to absorb rather than inflict violence, to embrace rather than deny suffering, and to endure in (rather than escape from) death.

Here exists an alternative understanding of 'freedom' not as random license but as disciplined commitment. Those who grasp at life lose it, says Jesus. Only those who are prepared to lose can gain, because what they are gaining is far greater than mere self-propagation.

Of course what makes this promise possible (and for many, impossible) is that, by definition, it can only arise from the unconstrained life of God, not from our own capabilities, fantasies and projections.

For this reason the God who exists beyond metaphysics and manipulation is met in a crucifixion brought about by religious and political power, not in the comforts of consumer 'spirituality' or in the self-regard of those who claim God as their own.

As the playwright Dennis Potter put it, on the threshold of his own death from cancer, "I have come to see that religion is the wound not the bandage." This is not the Gospel we thought we knew, but one given to us beyond our means, and indeed beyond our meanness.

A new vision of 'church'

To be authentically 'church' is to be the community made possible by this realisation. It is to open up an encounter with those who are different to us. It is to be possessed by the crazy idea that chaos, conflict and contract are not the only possible renderings of diversity. There is covenant towards communion too.

Rescue (salvation) is the unspeakable necessity that meets us in the Gospel as we consider what this hope really requires, however. We cannot do it on our own. We need to be radically changed, personally and politically.

The baptism we are offered, through death to life, is the means for this. It is not a reduction into a narrow, self-affirming, life-denying sect, as many preach and believe today. Rather it is slow, continuous transformation within a community of welcome and rejection, gathering and dispersal.

We welcome people, but we reject what degrades and divides. We gather in as the Body broken and renewed, but we receive that brokenness and renewal in the world, not in our favoured religious hiding places.

At the heart of this *ekklesia*, the assembled and sent-out community, is prayer. This is the language of donation through which we understand that the life we share is given to us, not possessed by us.

Similarly, worship is the means to identify whose we are and what is really worshipful (worth-it-full). It is this that forms us in the face of masses of things that claim dominion over our humanity: money, possessions, status, allure, xenophobia, violence, greed and self-absorption.

The fruit of the Gospel community, then, is not exclusion but embrace, not detachment but engagement, not credulity but critical thought. This is extremely difficult for Christians in a world where they have been offered, and taken, power along the lines of the 'religious right' in the United States.

To be people of God is to lose this dangerous desire to 'be in control' and to recognise the significance of not being finally determined by who we are and what we do. This is what is meant by 'being made in the image of God'.

So the challenge to the conventionally religious of Jesus' day was to abandon a fearful misreading of their rituals, texts and institutions – the one that enabled them to condemn those who God loves: strangers, the poor, the excluded, the odd, the 'unclean' and the marginalised.

This is also the challenge in our day. Those who turn God into a sentimental sop for their own egos or into a tyrannical buttress for their own interests are not walking Jesus' path. His is a road where you will find strangers and enemies, outcasts and friends – all those invited into the Feast of Life.

Reconciling difference or reviving exclusivism?

This, then, is the Gospel's radical portrait of what is involved in reconciling difference. And what are the alternatives? One is the superpower heresy that enables us to project all the evil 'out there' and to seek to bomb or suppress it into submission. That isn't Christianity, it's Manicheanism.

Another is the kind of religion that turns love into hatred, God into a despot, and faith into a revoltingly pious exercise in self-delusion. It doesn't matter much whether it quotes the Bible, the Qur'an, the Bhagavad-Gita or the Buddha, for it is blinded by what it preaches.

A third is that distortion of empiricism, positivism and rationalism which says humans are nothing more than the sum of their own parts. This is a self-constructed 'whole' that leaves us tragically bereft of the actual resources that are on offer if the Gospel is anything like true.

The challenge, of course, is that this Gospel does not allow us to write off the 'others' of religious and secular fundamentalism, either. In the face of hate and death-dealing, Jesus embodied the difficult, narrow call to shared life – and paid the price. To be a disciple of his is to live by the conviction that his death is not the end of hope, but its beginning.

If we took this message seriously and joyfully others might still think us bonkers. But at least we Christians might have something worth calling Good News on our hands. That's much better than colluding with the appalling betrayals of religion that lead from 'faith' to fratricide, from 'curing' to killing.

Note:

This article first appeared on Ekklesia, and on the Bruderhof website, in January 2005. It was revised slightly in May 2008.

Chapter Two

Choosing to be a house or a ship

Glynn Cardy

Here's Matthew. Sitting at his tax booth, doing his extorting best, like the good little Roman lackey he was. Along breezes Jesus. "Hey, you, follow me!" The breeze lifts him up, picks him up, snaps the mooring ropes, and he's away.

Away to where? Well, Matthew didn't have a clue. All he knew was that transformative power in Jesus had filled his sails and his heart. But he didn't know where he was bound. Neither did Jesus.

The Christian church, like other world religions, attracts adherents by its perceived stability. In a world that seems to be constantly in flux it is a religion that has endured 2,000 years. Each week in the marketplace ideas, structures, products, and processes are hailed as 'new' and 'better', as if those two adjectives are synonymous. And each week, contra the marketplace, a number find comfort in grounding their spirituality in traditions and rites dating back centuries. With magnificent buildings made to endure, Christianity declares to the world that at least here permanence is presumed. No fickle wind, whim, or scandal is going to change the church.

The common model for this understanding of Christianity is that of a house. Built on the 'sure foundation' of Jesus Christ, as one popular hymn attests, this house will supposedly endure forever. Grounded in the Bible and tradition this rock-solid structure will be able to withstand the storms of change and doubt.

Much of the debate within Christianity is between those who want to reinforce the foundations, strengthen the walls, and keep foreign winds and doctrines out, and those who want to open the windows and doors to the world and be prepared to change time-honoured methods and ideas in order to do so.

Both sides are using the model of house. The critical issue is the limits of hospitality, how accommodating the church should be. The debate about homosexual clergy and blessings, for example, is in part a debate about how open the doors of the house can be without compromising the foundations of the whole building.

God, in the house model, is at best a benevolent tolerant host who opens the gates to strangers, welcomes them and dines with them. God may take on board the strangers' suggestions about rearranging the furniture, even knocking a hole in a wall, but the basic foundations and structure will remain unchanged. For God in this model is not only the host but also in charge of the property. Order and structure, the look of permanence, remains immutable.

This is the model of church and God that most often passes for Christianity. There are, though, Christians who are not comfortable with this model. They tire of the 'in-house' debates, like the one over lesbian and gay clergy and blessings, not because the issues are unimportant, but because the model is not true to their experience of God, faith, and community.

A building doesn't move. It isn't meant to. The model assumes that the land won't move either. It is essentially a static model, supportive of the illusion of an unchanging past and a predictable future. It assumes that any change is peripheral to community, faith, and, of course, God.

Some of these discontented Christians articulate their faith and understanding of the church by using the rather different, but also biblical, model of a ship. The late Brazilian archbishop Helder Camara [see note 2 below], for example, once wrote:

"Pilgrim: when your ship, long moored in harbour, gives you the illusion of being a house; when your ship begins to put down roots in the stagnant water by the quay: put out to sea! Save your boat's journeying soul, and your own pilgrim soul, cost what it may."

The courage to change

If one considers the church to be more like a ship than a house then nearly everything changes. The Bible ceases to be a brick to fortify your structure or throw at your enemy, but is spiritual food for the journey. It gives energy for the challenges ahead. So does other 'food' – like the collective wisdom of other cultures. The traditions of the church are not a legal system but a guide, helping with the little tasks, teaching for example the theory of the helm but not doing the steering.

God too changes. Instead of being the gracious host and property overseer, God is the wind in one's sails and the beat in one's heart. God is a power within more than a power without, but not limited by either boundary. God is the energy of transformative love.

This wind of God is more a breaker of rules than a maker of rules. It is less interested in order and structure, than in those excluded from order and structure. Change is not a threat, inconvenience, or prescription, but part of its nature. It is a God that refuses to be tamed.

The house church and the ship church have very different attitudes to leaks. Leaks in the church can be thought of as the things that go wrong, the plans that don't quite work out, and the hurt people who distribute their hurt around. In a house a leak needs urgent attention. It drips on your head and can rot your walls. It needs to be repaired before your dinner guests arrive, or are even invited. In a ship, however, a leak is expected. Bilge pumps are normative. You don't stop the ship to attend to them, unless they are very serious. Leaks are part of sailing.

Yet the biggest difference between the two models of church and God is risk. The house, even an open house, speaks of security, stability, and safety. The inhabitants know where they are, what to expect, and even whom they might meet at the door. The ship, on the other hand, is heading out into unknown waters. The familiar towns and headlands are no longer there. The good old ways become more irrelevant day by day. God, faith, and community have or will change. They will also become more essential; more connected with the essence of each person aboard.

Like St Paul tossed around on the sea of Adria, St Matthew, long ago, boarded a ship and left the surety of his vocation, the known markers of his business, culture, religion, and God in the house of Judaism; and headed out to sea.

The church where I serve in Auckland, New Zealand bears St Matthew's name. On some days we are house-focused: rightly concerned about the institution of Christianity – its squabbles, the debates over the nature of its foundations, and how open are its doors – and it consumes our thoughts and prayers. However on most days, with no disrespect to the house that nurtured us, we are out sailing.

We are looking to the horizon and the horizon is looking at us. Our website statistics tell us that many thousands of new and unique visitors come to us each month. Some are looking for a house and its God; but not many. Most are looking for a different hope, a different way of church that includes their difference, and a different way of envisioning and experiencing God. And that's what we seek to offer.

The message from the church should not be 'get stuck in concrete', it should be 'welcome aboard.'

Notes

1. This reflection was specifically prepared for St Matthew's Day. Glynn Cardy's other writings are available online at: http://www.stmatthews.org.nz/nav.php?sid=74

2. Dom Helder Camara, A Thousand Reasons For Living (Darton, Longman and Todd, 1981).

3. In the Bible there are metaphors, stories and pictures to guide people that involve rock and foundations. There is a place for being solid. But far the greater number are to do with fluidity (baptism), openness to the prompting of the Spirit (likened to a 'mighty wind'), Jesus accompanying frightened disciples in the boat, walking on water, sailing forth, pilgrimage, journeying and sojourning. It is these we urgently need to recover in the contemporary church (whether we use a large or a small 'c').

Chapter Three

Opening ourselves to wisdom

Savitri Hensman

'Anyone of discretion acts by the light of knowledge,' wrote the ancient author of Proverbs. Many people of faith highly value study and work diligently to deepen their understanding, in a spirit of humility and compassion. However others are less open, either because they are supremely confident that their own views are superior to any alternatives or because they fear that too much questioning will undermine faith or offend the Almighty. They may indeed undertake some learning, but within tightly restricted boundaries. Some even try to silence or expel dissenters.

Current tensions among Anglicans to some extent reflect these differences of approach. Until quite recently in this denomination, the quest for knowledge tended to be rated highly. Even if there was vigorous disagreement on particular matters, there was some measure of trust that the church, if open to the guidance of the Holy Spirit, would be led towards truth and justice. Yet some leaders now not only refuse to consider scholarship which does not conform to their own perspective but also demand the right to prohibit others from acting on the fruits of study.

This is a sharp break with mainstream Anglicanism. 'It is no part of the purpose of the Scriptures to give information on those themes which are the proper subject matter of scientific enquiry, nor is the Bible a collection of separate oracles, each containing a final declaration of truth. The doctrine of God is the centre of its teaching,' bishops from different parts of the world agreed at the 1930 Lambeth Conference. 'We believe that the work of our Lord Jesus Christ is continued by the Holy Spirit, who not only interpreted him to the Apostles, but has in every generation inspired and guided those who seek truth.' And 'We recognise in the modern discoveries of science - whereby the boundaries of knowledge are extended, the needs of men are satisfied and their sufferings alleviated - veritable gifts of God, to be used with thankfulness to him, and with that sense of responsibility which such thankfulness must create.'

The freedom of knowledge

In 1958, the Lambeth Conference gratefully acknowledged 'our debt to the host of devoted scholars who, worshipping the God of Truth, have enriched and deepened our understanding of the Bible, not least by facing with intellectual integrity the questions raised by modern knowledge and modern criticism', and 'the work of scientists in increasing man's knowledge of the universe, wherein is seen the majesty of God in his creative activity. It therefore calls upon Christian people both to learn reverently from every new disclosure of truth, and at the same time to bear witness to the biblical message of a God and Saviour apart from whom no gift can be rightly used.'

At that time, scientific knowledge and theological reflection on human sexuality, including close reading of the Old and New Testament, were developing rapidly. Attitudes among Anglicans to contraception had changed radically, and theologians were beginning to question whether the Bible had been correctly interpreted and whether same-sex partnerships were always wrong. The growing visibility of lesbian, gay and bisexual people in many urban centres throughout the world made it harder to ignore their concerns and the issues for faith communities as they prayed, worshipped, cared for those in need and sought to discern God's will.

In 1978, while heterosexuality was affirmed as the Scriptural norm, the Lambeth Conference explicitly recognised 'the need for deep and dispassionate study of the question of homosexuality, which would take seriously both the teaching of Scripture and the results of scientific and medical research. The Church, recognising the need for pastoral concern for those who are homosexual, encourages dialogue with them. (We note with satisfaction that such studies are now proceeding in some member Churches of the Anglican Communion.)' This was affirmed again by Lambeth 1988, which urged that such study and reflection 'take account of biological, genetic and psychological research being undertaken by other agencies, and the socio-cultural factors that lead to the different attitudes in the provinces of our Communion'.

By the 1998 Lambeth Conference, Anglicans in some dioceses had been engaged in prayerful reflection, serious study and discussion on these matters for twenty to forty years, and in some cases had come to rethink their views. Others refused even to begin. For instance in 1997, a theologically ultra-conservative Statement was adopted at an international conference in Kuala Lumpur, in the province of Southeast Asia. The Archbishop of Southeast Asia, Moses Tay, wrote, 'Refusal to accept homosexuality as sinful is a diabolical contradiction of the Word of God, and is a blatant attempt to destroy the Gospel of Salvation through Jesus Christ. This is an issue of eternal life and eternal death. It is not a matter of opinion or a subject for study by an appointed commission. It is my conviction that faithful people of God must unite and stand against current proposals to appoint commissions to study the issue or the Kuala Lumpur Statement. Such a wily approach must be resisted at all cost if we are to remain faithful to Scripture and resist the temptation of the devil who tempted Eve to use her intellect against the Word of God in the same way.'

Openness to the voice of the Spirit

While caution is indeed important in approaching new developments and discoveries (and rediscoveries), and theories should be tested rigorously, those who ignore or suppress the fruits of study in fact put huge confidence not in divine truth but in their own intellects, assuming it is impossible that they might be wrong. Yet no human is intellectually infallible. It is all too easy to end up 'teaching human precepts as doctrines' (Mark 7.7).

In contrast, careful investigation and meaningful dialogue, in the context of mercy towards fellow-creatures and humility before God, can help sift out what is of value from what is poorly argued or based on incorrect data, and enable the church to be open to the workings of the Holy Spirit. And if indeed people are in the right, they are more likely to convince others if they engage with the arguments rather than simply insisting that they themselves are correct.

In addition, by the late 1990s, in some communities, the credibility of the church was at stake. Many theologians had by then come to believe that same-sex relationships were not always contrary to God's will. Old and New Testament scholars, church historians, academics of many denominations had contributed to the debate. This resonated with the experience of many Anglicans seeking to live out their faith and witness to the good news in the context of parish life. Other theologians were unconvinced but could at least demonstrate that they had thought seriously about the issues. However certain church leaders, who made a point of not studying deeply, and then made sweeping claims which contradicted the experience of many lesbians and gays and their families and friends, were less than plausible when they claimed to be champions of truth and morality.

Some senior clergy, for instance, loudly insisted that everyone was naturally heterosexual and same-sex attraction was the result of wilful wickedness. This was out of keeping with the reality with which many people within and outside the church were familiar. These leaders' approach to the Bible too left many Christians uneasy, as if it were merely a prop for their own views rather than a rich spiritual resource which might disturb and challenge them as well as others.

There were indeed provinces where, quite understandably, detailed work on human sexuality had been delayed because of other pressing concerns such as civil war, yet where there was openness to new knowledge. Elsewhere, certain leaders did not even pretend to be willing to consider seriously perspectives other than their own.

Voices of fear and anger

'This is the voice of God talking. Yes, I am violent against sin. Sodom and Gomorrah were destroyed,' shouted the Bishop of Enugu, Nigeria, trying to exorcise the general secretary of the Lesbian and Gay Christian Movement outside the conference hall at Lambeth. (The Bishop was probably unaware of the detailed work by various scholars examining what the sin of Sodom actually was.) Yet one of the founding principles of Anglicanism had been that no man could claim the authority to speak with the voice of God.

After a heated debate largely dominated by those dismissive of the value of study and dialogue, the 1998 Lambeth Conference adopted a resolution which took a relatively conservative position on sexuality but again affirmed the need for a listening process. This was upheld in the flawed but influential Windsor Report a few years later, when divisions had deepened.

Yet so deep is the aversion of some bishops to the notion of deep and dispassionate study and genuine dialogue that this is usually treated as an optional extra. For example, calls to discipline leaders who do not abide by the 1998 resolution on sexuality or the Windsor Report almost invariably refer to those who have moved too far in accepting partnered gays and lesbians. It is as if the sections of these documents which advocate investigating matters carefully and listening to different experiences and perspectives had not been written. Perhaps 'insistence upon the duty of thinking and learning as essential elements in the Christian life' (Lambeth 1930) has become so outrageous a demand as to be unthinkable. And now those who have not bothered to examine the issues in any depth, and who have in some cases persecuted people in their own provinces who have tried to promote in-depth study and meaningful dialogue, are demanding that their own power be extended to other parts of the world.

After the Windsor Report, many clerical and lay leaders in North America were willing to postpone further steps towards full inclusion, painful though this was; but hardliners scornfully rejected such concessions. They wanted nothing less than submission to them. This was too much for many Anglicans who wished to 'seek and serve Christ' in all people, 'loving your neighbour as yourself' (in the words of the baptismal liturgy used in some parts of the church). There seemed little point in continuing to wait if genuine dialogue was not happening.

Some of those eager to move forward had not studied the issues in much depth. However there were also numerous people who, at first, had taken the line that only heterosexual relationships leading to marriage should be supported, but who had come – after much study, thought and prayer – to change their minds. Yet they were accused of acting hastily and being guided simply by social mores. In other denominations, too, there were tensions between those who felt that love of God and faithfulness to their tradition involved willingness to delve deeply into difficult matters such as human sexuality and others who felt that the inheritance they were called on to preserve meant unquestioning adherence to certain beliefs on family life.

A family of deep learning?

Thought-provoking theological work on the theology of sexuality and the family, in the context of faith in the Trinity and pursuit of the kingdom of heaven, continues to be done. Many Christians are no more aware of this than of the writings of theologians such as Derrick Sherwin Bailey in the 1950s, Helmut Thielicke in the 1960s or John J McNeill in the 1970s. From their point of view, it is outrageous that what they have taken for granted on such an emotive issue as human sexuality should be questioned, and doing so would open the floodgates.

The controversy which has arisen over this particular issue reveals wider differences. It is hard today to imagine that the 1968 Lambeth Conference (not unlike other Christian gatherings around the same time) could,

'having considered and welcomed

(a) the increasing extent of human knowledge,

(b) the prospect of human control of the natural environment,

(c) the searching enquiries of the theologians, calls the Church to a faith in the living God which is adventurous, expectant, calm, and confident, and to faith in the standards of Christ, who was, and is, and is to come, as the criterion of what is to be welcomed and what is to be resisted in contemporary society.'

The importance of thoughtful and prayerful study, in which different perspectives are weighed up before conclusions are reached, is greater than ever before, not only for scholars and bishops but also for laypeople and parish clergy in communities across the world. Poverty and preventable disease continue to cause terrible suffering, while ecological disaster, militarism, violent nationalism and religious hatred threaten the very survival of humankind. How can the hungry be fed, the homeless sheltered, the sick healed, death-dealing divisions be overcome? How are the extremes of misogyny, ethnic supremacism, homophobia, child abuse and disdain for those who are poor, disabled or unemployed connected with milder forms of prejudice and snobbery, and how can destructive forces most effectively tackled? Is bullying in the family, playground, workplace and organisation best dealt with by giving in to the demands of those who misuse power and, if not, how can such behaviour be firmly yet lovingly confronted?

Some may be tempted to shy away from thinking too deeply about such matters, trusting in politicians or church leaders to tell them what to think. There is also a trend in some church circles towards emphasising the authority of bishops, and 'unity' based on dominance. Yet 'ordinary' Christians cannot shrug off their responsibility to strive to follow Christ and love others as God loves them, which includes seeking to understand and address the issues profoundly affecting families, neighbourhoods, humankind and life on earth. Many in Anglican and ecumenical circles are taking seriously the need to learn from Scripture, tradition and reason and listen to the poor and excluded as well as the rich and respectable.

Hard work will be needed if the gulf which has opened up is to be bridged. Moves towards increasing the power of senior clergy, and their unaccountability to those they supposedly serve, will not help. Why should laypeople used to taking responsibility in other areas of life, and having to argue their case if they are to persuade others to take their views on board, passively accept the pronouncements of bishops who have not done their homework, especially if this undermines local mission and ministry?

Even in countries where top church leaders emphatically reject the value of listening and learning, many clergy and laypeople are far more realistic about human diversity than those in the hierarchy, and are eager to learn more about the complex universe which God has created. Indeed, developing and sharing knowledge may be an even more urgent task than in other, more secure and prosperous, countries. In time, pressure from below may prove most effective in fostering greater openness. Until then, unity is likely to be strained.

Part Two: Questioning

Chapter Four

Why do these Christians hate one another?

Simon Barrow

Christians, it has been said (in the Epistle to Diognetus and elsewhere), should be known by their love – by lives which show some glimpse of the fact that, in Christ, we have encountered a depth of relation and a vision of abundant living which enables us to strive against some other propensities of our creaturely condition: suspicion, competitiveness, the desire for vindication, and so on.

Sadly, it is all too easy to use our affiliations, including those that employ spiritual labels, in a different way. The contrast is brought out well – a correspondent commented to me recently – in the otherwise incidental juxtaposition of two headlines in Ekklesia's UK news briefing on 18 April 2007. Namely: "[Rowan] Williams says the Bible invites listening not dogmatism" followed immediately by "Dean's atonement talk resulted in abuse and obscenity."

The issue of contention was a radio talk given by the Anglican Dean of St Albans about the meaning of Christ's death on the Cross, which should be interpreted, he said, as an act of self-giving in confrontation with the forces of evil in our world, not as some kind of divinely sanctioned suicide or imposed 'vicarious' death.

I have a personal interest in this story. Though we don't know each other well, I overlapped with Jeffrey John, the Dean concerned, when we both worked in Southwark Anglican diocese in the 1990s. We were respectively involved in different aspects of theological education with lay people and clergy. I have considerable respect for Jeffrey's integrity as a scholar and as a Christian. As it happens, I also agree with him about depictions of the cross which wrongly turn God into a sadist.

But that isn't the point. The point is that the hate mail he received is far more disloyal to the community of Christ than any alleged problem it sought to address. No doubt many of his interlocutors informed the Dean of St Alban's (in between the insults and jibes – some to do with his sexuality) that they were "Bible believers".

But by turning the text they purported to honour into a weapon they were, in fact, soiling it. Blasphemy is not people saying rude things about Christianity (they might have good reason!), it is believers betraying the love that has called them.

Listening and hearing interpretatively

By contrast, what Dr Williams was seeking to get across in his lecture on listening and hearing interpretatively, is that to take the Bible and its message seriously is to receive the world it re-describes as part of a conversation: to understand ourselves first as "lovingly addressed" by God, and then to seek to put this into practice in the way we think and argue together as much as what we say.

He was also making the point that the manner in which we read texts – and not just biblical ones, either – is influenced by the overall shape of the story we inhabit. A life-changing narrative of forgiveness, peace, justice and continual reformation takes patience, nurture and good habits (of both heart and mind) cultivated around a table of friendship, the Gospel suggests.

It follows that there are no quick routes to knock-down meaning, whether in biblical interpretation, scientific exploration or any other field of enquiry. People, the world and God are not straightforward, simple and objectifiable; they are rich, dynamic and complex. And so are the texts which constitute the story of our encounters with them.

To "live by the book" is not to read off a series of propositions onto the template of our lives. It is to encounter a word of hope made flesh, conveyed in language and lived in history. In seeing the biblical narrative as 'inspired' (inhabited by the Spirit who "comforts the disturbed and disturbs the comfortable", as John Wesley nicely put it) we recognise that God's 'speech' is illuminative not overpowering.

In words I am often brought back to, Nicholas Lash puts it like this: "Good learning calls no less than teaching does, for courtesy, respect, a kind of reverence; reverence for facts and people, evidence and argument, for climates of speech and patterns of behaviour different from our own. There are, I think, affinities between the courtesy, the attentiveness, required for friendship; the passionate disinterestedness without which no good scholarly or scientific work is done; and the contemplativity which strains, without credulity, to listen for the voice of God - who speaks the Word [s]he is, but does not shout." ('Cacophany and Conversation', The 2002 Prideaux Lectures delivered at the University of Exeter)

Human beings as mysteries to be loved

It seems to me that the major "cultural accommodation" of modern Christianity is not that some of us now think there is a good case to be made for our gay sisters and brothers being seen as a gift of God, rather than the threatening abomination many "traditional societies" held them to be (isn't that the opposite of "going with the crowd"?). No, it is submission to the dominant idea that other people who are different to us are simply a problem to be disposed of, rather than "mysteries to be loved" (T. S. Eliot).

Of course I realise that this warning is as much addressed to myself, and to those who I have closest affinity with, as to anyone else. And that I fall short of my own admonition. But that's the point. Right interpretation is a function and feature of the development of right relation, which in turn requires some kind of honesty about one's own faults.

When St Paul suggested that we all sin and fall short of the glory of God, he wasn't issuing a call for self-loathing (as is easily supposed these days). He was modestly reminding us that we all mess things up. It isn't the case that some of us do, while others are unassailably right all the time. This liberating realisation is what Catholic theologian James Alison wonderfully calls "the joy of being wrong".

The culture of thinly disguised nastiness does not just apply to intra-Christian strife or to 'religious people', of course. It is a more general feature of public life. We say we want politicians to admit errors and apologise. But when they do so, we say they are weak and unfit for office – and we do so with little sense of irony or self-knowing. In the process any possibility of achieving common truthfulness is lost.

Disagreement is an unavoidable part of human development. Argument is a good thing. Suspicion towards power is vital. But without an understanding that we are held in love, these things lose a sense of proportion and can spill over into contempt or even hatred.

There is a story about a reclusive holy man who after a long period of prayer decides to go for a walk. He meets a stranger who begins to berate him about the evils of his faith. The man listens sympathetically until his verbal assailant demands to know: "How will you respond to these charges!" He thinks for a minute and says: "I'd be happy to discuss all this with you. But first we need to agree that we have no need to harm each other, that we can be friends. Otherwise anything I say will only add to your sense of injustice. And that matters to me more than being right."

Notes

1. 'Williams says the Bible invites listening not dogmatism', Ekklesia - http://www.ekklesia.co.uk/node/5071

2. 'Dean's atonement talk resulted in abuse and obscenity', Ekklesia - http://www.ekklesia.co.uk/node/5075

Chapter Five

Is lack of integrity losing the young?

Tim Nafziger

For many years now, high profile Christian leaders have been saying that homosexuality is destroying the church. It turns out that something like the opposite could in fact be the case. It may be that the homophobia of some church leaders is isolating the church and undermining opportunities for connecting with a new generation of non-Christians, the young especially.

According to a study in the USA carried out in 2007 by the Barna Group (an evangelical market research firm), perception of Christians among young non-Christians has nose-dived over the last decade, in ways that parallel what many say has been happening for some time in Europe. An article on Alternet reporting on the study notes that:

'Ten years ago, "the vast majority" of non-Christians [under 30] had generally favourable views of Christianity. Now, that number stands at just 16%. When asked specifically about Evangelicals, the numbers are even worse: only 3% of non-Christian Millennials have positive associations with Evangelicals.'

These changes didn't come out of the blue. The study found that the strongest negative trait associated with the church among non-Christians was an "anti-homosexual" one at 91%. A close second and third were being judgmental (87%) and being hypocritical (85%). According to the summary of the study, as outlined on Alternet:

'Non-Christians and Christians explained that beyond their recognition that Christians oppose homosexuality, they believe that Christians show excessive contempt and unloving attitudes towards gays and lesbians. One of the most frequent criticisms of young Christians was that they believe the church has made homosexuality a "bigger sin" than anything else.'

I am sure that many Christians will try to spin this as a result of increased 'persecution' of Christians in the United States or the influence of the secular, liberal media. But the study specifically highlights that perception is based on actual interactions with Christian friends or on attending church events.

A whopping 80% of non-Christians surveyed had spent at least six months going to church. These are not casual cynics, jaded by the media. They are people who have tried Christianity and found it wanting. In other words, all of us Christians are responsible. We cannot just point our fingers at some other part of the church or secular society. Where have we failed to model the radical hospitality of Jesus?

Faith in Jesus, but not the church

Although the study makes no mention of George W. Bush, I suspect that the years of his administration and the policies it has encouraged have also played a role. This study is focused on the United States, but I believe that on a global level, the numbers might be even worse. I have often been brought back to reflect upon the corrosive effect of Christianity's association with American foreign policy, something that I experienced first hand in England when I worked with the Anabaptist Network UK and in church-related conflict transformation.

But that corrosion is happening in my own country as well, and undoubtedly it has been a factor in there only being a 3% positive association with the term 'evangelical' among young non-Christians in the USA. Globally, people are even less likely to distinguish between George Bush's brand of evangelicalism and the rest of us who wear that label.

So where is the hope in all this? Recently, I started reading "Revolution in Jesusland", a blog by Zack Exley, the progressive political and social organiser, formerly of Moveon.org and GWbush. com. During the course of several weeks, Zack went from one Christian conference to another listening to the likes of Shane Claiborne lead 11,000 evangelicals in a 'Litany of Resistance'. His message is the title of his blog: Christians are beginning to discover that Jesus calls us to cross boundaries in revolutionary ways. While attending a Christian Community Development Association conference in St Louis, he declared:

'I've had friends who were the children of the Catholic Worker movement—whose parents moved into poor urban areas in the 60s. I remember thinking that must have been some dying gasp of the Christian progressive (then, socialist) movement. But, as it turns out, (conservative!) evangelical Christians picked up where that movement left off. A lot of these leaders moved in to their neighbourhoods starting in the 80s and 90s. And now the movement to move into "broken" neighbourhoods seems to be reaching a fever pitch. I don't have any stats to back that up, and I doubt anyone does. But it's the new must-do thing for Christians who are "on fire for Jesus."'

That is partly why I know I still have hope in Jesus Christ, who somehow remains remarkably popular among all sorts of people. The most common unprompted comment among those surveyed Barna was 'Christianity in today's society no longer looks like Jesus.' Everyone in American culture, Christian and non-Christian, seems to know deep down that our founder stands for peace, love and compassion.

I still remember watching a Daily Show TV episode where presenter Jon Stewart made an ironic comment comparing George Bush with Jesus. Everyone laughed. They understood the basic character of Jesus.

Do we?

Notes

1. See: 'A New Generation Expresses its Skepticism and Frustration with Christianity', 24 September 2007, The Barna Group - http://www.barna.org

2. Sara Robinson, 'Young People Rejecting Christianity, Have Perception of Religion as Homophobic', 10 October 2007, Alternet - http://www.alternet.org/blogs/peek/64873/

3. This article is a slightly edited version of one that appeared on Ekklesia, and initially on Young Anabaptist Radicals - http://young. anabaptistradicals.org/

Chapter Six

Life-changing hospitality

Deirdre J. Good

Back in 2007, on a trip to the United Kingdom (I live and work in the United States), I participated in a talk on hospitality at St Ethelburga's Centre for Reconciliation and Peace in London. I feel grateful to them for their gracious welcome. That talk and the subsequent discussion got me thinking about ways in which we speak about and practice hospitality – and how it challenges us in different ways, not least as Christians and custodians of church communities.

Any discussion about hospitality needs to be hospitable. How is a space welcoming? This particular discussion was conducted in a circle, which for many indicates inclusion. But people may choose to participate from beyond the circle for various reasons and we need to provide for that. We need to focus on the people to whom a welcome is shown, anticipating and facilitating their degrees of involvement in the event.

We can all agree that hospitality is a Christian virtue. But why are we thinking about hospitality at all? Hospitality is central to other religious traditions. Abraham's offering of food and protection to the three messengers of the Lord in Genesis 18 becomes the paradigm for ancient Israelite, Jewish, and early Christian hospitality. In fact, hospitality to strangers is a mandate in most non-Western societies. I've been welcomed into the houses of complete strangers in Matere Valley, Nairobi and in the favellas of San Paulo in ways that I would never be welcomed into the apartments of strangers in Manhattan.

Openness to strangers reflects a mindset most of us who are Western don't intrinsically possess. Is this why our discussions of hospitality can dwindle to stories of our hosting (non-Western) strangers in our homes? But if our discussions and practice of hospitality become questions of whom we welcome into our homes (and for how long under what conditions), then we have lost the dynamic of exchange that hospitality presupposes. Hospitality has become a one-way street. We determine who is invited and who is excluded because it is our home, our castle.

Such an interpretation is not about welcoming anyone - it is about control. Welcoming someone has become secondary to an assessment-a judgment by me as host about the kind of stranger that is welcome and the type of welcome that is appropriate. If we reduce hospitality to an arbitration of who is and who is not welcomed by us as hosts into our homes, and under what conditions, is this not a diminution of God's hospitality to the point of distortion?

I believe this is also true of debates about conditions and circumstances under which people may approach the communion table. If we enter into such debates, we have already decided that there is such a debate about who is welcome and who is not. I myself believe that on this question, the evidence of the gospels is univocal: Jesus practised open table fellowship with respect to God's hospitality. It wasn't his table. He was received as a stranger, welcomed as a guest, and gave hospitality at the tables of strangers or acquaintances. Sometimes he learnt from others about brokering God's limitless inclusion.

Relocating Christian practice

The practice of hospitality is not about being a good host: it is about participating in a continual exchange of the roles of stranger, guest and host. It presupposes a network of relationships-an awareness of interdependence. We can see this best in the story of the two disciples encountering a stranger on the road to Emmaus. That stranger walks and talks along the road with them about recent events in Jerusalem. They offer him hospitality at the end of the day whereupon, invited to stay as a guest, he assumes the position of host and is identified by them as he breaks bread.

On the road to Emmaus and in a place that is not his, a homeless, resurrected Jesus moves fluidly between roles of stranger, host and guest. Luke's Jesus offers Westerners the challenge of receiving and giving hospitality "to go." In Luke's gospel, journeys characterise and shape ministry; Jesus journeys to Jerusalem for most of the gospel while in Acts, disciples and apostles travel from Jerusalem to Samaria, to Europe, and eventually to Rome.

Hospitality facilitates and defines Jesus' journey to Jerusalem; it identifies followers and disciples who listen and extend welcome (Mary and Martha, the mission of the Seventy, the Good Samaritan, Zacchaeus) and solidifies opposition (some Pharisees and scribes).

When we relocate the practice of Christian hospitality from who is and who is not welcome in our homes to the recognition that hospitality is offered and received in other places along the way, a different more permeable dynamic opens up. But changing the location of the welcome is only half the solution. Offering someone food in a soup kitchen, while it is a good thing in itself, is not actually hospitality because it is not rooted in an exchange of roles.

Beyond familiarity

In post-biblical tradition, Abraham, the paradigm of hospitality, moves out of the familiarity of his house. He pitches a tent at the crossroads so as to welcome more strangers, according to the Testament of Abraham. Philo says Abraham ran out of his house and begged the strangers who were passing by his home to stay with him because he was so eager to extend hospitality to them.

Abraham and Jesus confront our restrictive notions of hospitality, encouraging us to think about our human interdependence in giving and receiving hospitality on the way.

Notes

1. This article first appeared on the Episcopal Café website of the Diocese of Washington (http://www.episcopalcafe.com/), and then on Ekklesia.

2. Episcopal Café is seeking to model a form of Gospel-based hospitality. Its originators explain: "The Café is collaborative effort by more than two dozen writers and editors, and an ever-growing list of visual artists. Together, we aspire to create a visually appealing, intellectually stimulating, spiritually enriching and at least occasionally amusing site where Episcopalians and those interested in our church can read, watch, listen and reflect upon contemporary life in a context informed by faith and animated by the spirit of charity.

"Our aim is frankly, but we hope gently, evangelical. To the extent that we can speak intelligently, passionately, persuasively and truthfully—and to the degree that we manifest wisdom, humility and genuine concern for those we disagree with—we will succeed in drawing Episcopalians more deeply into their faith, and in persuading those without a spiritual home to explore our Church."

Part Three: Hoping

Chapter Seven

Being Church in the freedom of God

Savitri Hensman

Worshipping a God who is more wonderful than humans can possibly imagine can be difficult. Almost inevitably, our minds seek something or someone within our experience to whom the Divine might be likened, linked perhaps with how we relate to God individually and collectively.

The Bible offers numerous metaphors – a rock, a dove, a mighty warrior, a woman searching for a lost coin and so forth – and the abundance and variety can remind us not to take any of these, including their gender designations, literally. The heavenly Father does not have hormones and the living Water will not freeze at low temperatures! Theologians, artists, musicians and poets have further added to the rich store of images which reflect one or another facet of the Divine, and which help humankind to delight in and respond to the generosity and love lavished on us.

This is not to say that all images of God are equally valid. For example the 'prosperity gospel' approach which teaches that wealth and comfort are evidence of God's favour, as if God were a superhuman version of, and inspiration to, those living in luxury while their neighbours go short of the necessities of life, is a travesty of the good news of Jesus Christ.

However it is tempting but risky to underestimate the complexity, from a human viewpoint, of expressing and representing God's unsurpassable nature; and, perhaps unconsciously, it is easy to give too much weight to a particular way of trying to comprehend the Divine. This may be an idealised version of a certain kind of leader – perhaps a feudal monarch who is generous to those who submit to him but harsh to his foes, the head of a household or the wise and charismatic chief executive of a large non-governmental organisation empowering volunteers to do good – and of a framework where such leadership can be exercised.

There may be an element of truth in such a picture: if humans learn to love (however imperfectly) through being loved by God and wisdom is a gift from 'on high', something about the Divine may be learnt from observing leaders when they act in a wise and compassionate manner. But even the greatest person is finite and fallible.

Crucially, God may also be glimpsed in those with little power and prestige, if humankind as a whole is made in God's image (Genesis 1.27) and whatever we do to the least of our brothers and sisters we do to Christ (Matthew 25.31-46). Indeed if Jesus is like a servant (Luke 22.27), and whoever has seen him has seen the Father (John 14.8-10), this turns conventional notions of divinity and glory upside down. For most of us, used to worldly notions of greatness, it may be easier to imagine God as a power-wielding patriarch than as an anguished mother hen whose chicks reject her nurturing (Matthew 23.37) or as a convict awaiting execution. Yet in fact the King wears a crown of thorns, and far from endorsing power mongers, he is crucified by them.

Imposing institutional limits on God

Since the early days of the church, there has been a tendency to create institutional structures and to define the bounds of what could be said about God. While valuable in some ways in enabling Christians to coordinate what they do and be clear about what they believe, this has drawbacks. It may foster power-struggles as different individuals and factions strive for supremacy or try to stay in favour with the winners, as tends to happen in any institution. And the imposition of rules and codes, if these are experienced as oppressive, instead of binding believers together in harmony may cause resentment and provoke strife.

What is more, even well-meaning attempts to discourage fellow-Christians from holding erroneous beliefs may themselves lead to error if a particular way of imagining and relating to the Divine is held up as a fixed norm, and other approaches are dismissed as heretical even if they may contain partial truths. In the course of debate, those with different perspectives may come to understand one another better and perhaps refine their own views. But if an ecclesiastical elite (often dominated by a particular faction) holds power and tries to enforce what it regards as true, serious difficulties may arise.

It is of course impossible to avoid offending everyone. White people with racist tendencies, for instance, may feel that the presence of black people in 'their' church is an imposition, though they may try to rationalise this. The image of a God who is white only may have been instilled into them at an impressionable age, and they may never have come to realise the beauty of One who can be imagined in diverse forms but contained by none of them.

Likewise there are some 'traditionalists' who are offended by female or maternal images of God. These images are a definite minority in the biblical tradition, but they are there. They have re-emerged in recent liturgy and theological writing as a corrective to naïve uses of 'Father' which do not appear to recognise its metaphorical construction, or which have been employed to justify patriarchal domination. (Commentators have pointed out that, rightly understood, construing fatherhood in relation to God, who is beyond limit, may call into question, rather than reinforce, patriarchal notions of the role of father.)

Debate not decree

Church leaders can indeed play an important part in confronting discriminatory attitudes and practices, but are likely to be most effective in the long term if they engage with those with whom they strongly disagree, explaining and debating rather than simply issuing fiat-like decrees. And sometimes it is senior clergy who lag behind, and who can learn from those 'below' them in the church hierarchy (one example being the abolition of the transatlantic slave trade, which many bishops opposed).

An authoritarian system supposedly intended to preserve church order and protect the truth can end up trying to control not only people but also God, as if God's graciousness could be regulated by the church. 'Ordinary' Christians and local congregations may learn to devalue their own encounters with the Divine, the insights they gain and what they learn about their calling unless these fit a pattern which has been authorised by those at the top. This may appeal not only to leaders but also to those laypeople and junior clergy who value conformity and predictability. Freedom, while valuable (2 Corinthians 3.17), can be challenging (Galatians 5.1).

A particular means of grace or concept of God may be enshrined as if it fully represented the truth, thus becoming an idol. So it may turn into an obstacle rather than an aid to encountering the living God, who continually goes beyond what humans expect. And idols can require human sacrifice (Ezekiel 23.36-39), as well as being powerless to save (Isaiah 45.20).

The institutional church can become an idol, its own interests and apparent unity taking priority over almost everything else. This may be rationalised as necessary to protect the faith of 'simple folk', obedience to the Biblical emphasis on unity – though to St Paul, for instance, valuing unity (Ephesians 4.1-6) certainly did not mean shying away from vigorous debate (Ephesians 4.15-16, 5.10-11) – or an imitation of the mutual love of the Holy Trinity, as if it were unloving to challenge acts of cruelty and cowardice which stunt faith and damage humanity.

The cover-up of child abuse by clergy (a problem in various denominations) is an example of how such an approach can backfire on leaders and institutions as well as causing great harm to individuals, families and the church's witness.

In the mid-twentieth century, it might have seemed that the days of rigid systems of church order and strictly-enforced boundaries of acceptable belief were coming to an end. In future, perhaps, differences would be settled not by the edicts of a small group of powerful men but rather by wide discussion and the opportunity to compare the fruits of different approaches to theology, liturgy and organisational matters (Matthew 7.15-20). The quest for truth would be aided by the Holy Spirit (John 16.13), poured out on even the lowliest so that they could discern and speak of wonderful things (Joel 2.28-29).

This is not to say that Christians of the day were starting from a blank slate: the Bible, the Creeds, liturgy, influential texts, commonly-used prayers and hymns had decisively helped to shape who they were, and served as an inspiration and guide. The ferment of discussion meant that ideas – whether from senior church people and approved theologians or little-known thinkers and previously marginalised communities – were often tested rigorously in the course of debate, and poorly constructed arguments or wild speculation challenged.

The cross as subversive, not conformist

In a flourishing of creativity during the Renaissance, great artists had depicted a flesh-and-blood Jesus, as vivid as if he had just been delivered by a local midwife or had stepped into a nearby market. Now Jesus was being drawn and painted in many different forms, not only as European-looking, the Divine incarnate amidst people of every nation, ethnicity, class and gender.

The ecumenical movement was flourishing, founded on an acknowledgement that Christians who did things differently were not necessarily scoundrels to be fought or fools to be pitied and maybe converted. There was an increasing willingness not to write off other forms of Christianity – perhaps the Baptist in a plain church building, the Anglo-Catholic amidst statues and clouds of incense and the Pentecostal swaying and clapping in a borrowed hall, and the Anabaptist holding all things in common and refusing to resist violently really were reaching towards the same Saviour! The winds of change blew over even the highly centralised Roman Catholic Church, which convened the groundbreaking Second Vatican Council in the early 1960s.

In many ways, things have gone backwards since then: the drive for 'purity' and centralisation of power in the Anglican Communion, say, is symptomatic of a wider trend. This may be due as much to an embrace of some of the more troubling aspects of the modern world as a rejection of it by those hankering after a largely imagined golden age, when the Bible or tradition supposedly held sway, and troubling problems could be referred to authoritative men in black suits or flowing robes.

How can churches 'market' themselves amidst strong competition from other denominations, religions and organisations? What kind of 'brand' is it they offer if their members worship a nameless, formless God who has been, and continues to be, experienced and followed in a myriad ways? How on earth can product recognition be achieved? And what chance is there of viable business strategies, let alone the prospect of mergers and acquisitions, if the chief executives or boards of directors cannot exercise international control over local branches?

The cross is indeed a globally recognised symbol, but what if it is seen not as a logo or talisman but rather as a reminder of a God who confounds expectations, mixes with the powerless and disreputable and gets into such trouble with the religious and political authorities that they exercise capital punishment, yet who will not stay safely buried? In trying to make God more marketable and manageable, what is most attractive, valuable and liberating about Christianity may be lost or driven underground.

The changing struggle within Anglicanism

Forty years ago the worldwide Anglican Communion, for all its faults, was widely associated with the valuing of Scripture, tradition and reason, the encouragement of scholarship in an atmosphere of intellectual freedom, provincial autonomy and recognition of the important role of laypeople. What emerged from the struggles of local Christian communities to hear and live the good news in their own context might not be adequately recognised by others, but could not be easily suppressed by senior clergy living thousands of miles away.

Sometimes there were hurt feelings when members of one party or faction felt that their own views were not given enough weight, and some of the ideas and practices which emerged seemed strange, even offensive, to those of other theological and liturgical persuasions. But innovations not led by the Holy Spirit tend, in time, to fizzle out, while more inspired developments spread.

At times, the most extreme Evangelicals and Anglo-Catholics, 'liberals' and 'conservatives' had some very unflattering things to say about each other's beliefs and rituals! However, those who were less partisan had the chance, in time, to expand their own horizons. And Anglicanism, through the wide variety of ways that God was perceived and worshipped, pointed to the truth that the Divine was greater than any human concept – an important lesson for today's world.

Now major divisions have become apparent as certain leaders convinced of their own correctness have demanded that supposedly erroneous practices in other (geographically-organised) provinces be stamped out, and some moderates have agreed to this, largely in order to persuade hardliners not to leave. In the course of the controversy, a small group of Primates (the most senior bishops in provinces) have taken unprecedented power, and the drive for centralisation continues.

Covenant, commitment and freedom

Early in 2007, a Primates' meeting began consulting on a draft Covenant in which provincial leaders would promise to 'uphold and act in continuity and consistency with the catholic and apostolic faith, order and tradition, biblically derived moral values and the vision of humanity received by and developed in the communion of member Churches', and express willingness 'to seek the guidance of the Instruments of Communion, where there are matters in serious dispute among churches that cannot be resolved by mutual admonition and counsel'; those who did not submit to their judgement would risk sanctions. (Three of the four bodies which bring Anglicans together internationally, the 'Instruments of Communion', are made up entirely of bishops.)

Though responses from some provinces have indicated profound misgivings about a Covenant of this kind, the Archbishop of Canterbury, Rowan Williams, a strong believer in church unity, is pushing ahead. In an Advent letter in December 2007, he made it clear that those attending the Lambeth Conference of bishops which he is convening in 2008 should be willing to endorse the notion of a Covenant which would 'avoid the present degree of damaging and draining tension arising again'. He also urged that bishops, rather than synods on which other clergy and laypeople are represented, should take 'responsibility for sustaining doctrinal standards'.

Later that month, a leading figure in the drive for greater centralisation, The Rev Dr Michael Poon from Singapore, chair of a Theological Formation and Education Task Force created by the hard-line Global South Anglican coalition, wrote of the extensive work this Task Force had put into 'a draft of the theological framework for an Anglican catechism', which would be 'a unitive and building document for the whole Communion' which 'would complement the GSA theological input to the Anglican Covenant processes. We took particular care in defining orthodoxy in the Anglican Communion in the document', which 'has important ramifications for Christian discipleship throughout the Communion'.

Divisions have opened up within the ranks of those seeking to impose their own version of doctrinal orthodoxy on the Anglican Communion on how this can best be achieved, with much debate over the wisdom of organising a Global Anglican Future Conference in Jerusalem which many see as a rival to the Lambeth Conference. However another leading light in this movement, the Rev Professor Stephen Noll, now based in Uganda, suggested in January 2008 that 'Strategically the idea of a Covenant is a good one' and urged that 'Those attending the Global Anglican Future Conference should maintain ties with those orthodox leaders who are working on the Communion Covenant.

It seems unlikely that a final Covenant from Canterbury, filtered now through the Anglican Consultative Council, will be sufficiently crisp to deal with the present crisis. However, the opportunity may arise hereafter to negotiate an ecumenical Anglican Covenant that will serve as a means of warding off heresy and will chart the future of orthodox Anglicanism.' Once the principle of a Covenant is established, it can be revised to be more restrictive.

God is God, not just 'our' God

While there is clearly much politicking going on in Anglican circles, there are some leaders who sincerely believe that enforcing what they regard as orthodoxy would be good for the church. However, their own beliefs and practices might be regarded by many other Anglicans as unorthodox, maybe even heretical.

Even if there were a far greater degree of agreement on 'orthodox Anglicanism' than currently exists, there would be problems in wording a Covenant and catechism which could be used to judge the acceptability of what people say and do in future. God is greater than any human concept or formula, tenderly intimate and compassionate in dealing with humankind but also unspeakably strange.

Attempts by church hierarchies to ban incorrect ideas and ensure that only suitably 'holy' or ideologically sound candidates are chosen as leaders may make some people feel more comfortable. Yet while greater strictness may prevent certain kinds of heresy, it may foster others, and there is a risk that worshippers may in some cases end up paying homage to a lifeless idol rather than the living God. And the witness of the church will be damaged, in a divided world where fanatical beliefs in distorted images of God or in 'market forces' and nationalist extremism wreak such havoc and threaten even greater destruction.

Yet God is not confined by rules set by humans, however powerful they may be by earthly standards, and is at work outside as well as within institutions. Wonderful things will continue to happen even if at first they are not acknowledged by the authorities, and in time truth will break through our illusions.

Notes

1. This chapter was first published as a research paper for Ekklesia under the title 'Binding the church and constraining God'.

2. See also Glynn Cardy's chapter, 'The Journey from House to Ship'.

Chapter Eight

Jesus and the transformation of family

Deidre J. Good

Modern families are being transformed: since 2005, statistics show that more women in America live by themselves and married couples now are in a minority. Similar trends can be observed in Britain and in other parts of Europe.

Our daughters, nieces and grandchildren are growing up into a world where being single will be normal at least for longer periods of time. The social and economic implications of this new situation include the reality that single women are heads of households.

Christian commentators who see a nuclear family as normative might want to describe this new reality as evidence of a further decline in family values. In fact, this new family configuration pries open a discussion of what family values were in Jesus' time and how to discern and appropriate New Testament material.

Just as we seek guidance in scriptures that are thousands of years removed from us, the actors and authors in those writings also sought guidance in their scriptures and showed us how. Paul is a prime example of this; he honours the scripture by wrestling with it, and while some of his interpretative manoeuvres are opaque to us, his intention to be responsible to scripture shines through clearly.

We cannot responsibly excise bits of scripture or deny what they meant in their own context, insofar as the meaning is accessible to us. But we can study the patterns of scripture, the direction of scripture, the underlying major themes in scripture, and bring those to bear on the interpretation of those passages which seem confined to the time and place when they were first written.

Households and relations

Among the oldest parts of the New Testament, Paul's letters commend "staying as you are" in light of impending apocalyptic catastrophe. For this reason, Paul counsels the Corinthian community in single-minded devotion to the Lord over and above the exercise of passion for which marriage is the containment. To community members whom he calls "brothers (and sisters)" Paul commends humility, patient affection, and competition in honouring each person in the body of Christ, that is, "sober judgment."

After Paul, the authors of the "household codes" counsel wives, children, and slaves to obey their husbands, fathers and masters. The author of Ephesians borrows the analogy of Christ and the church, enjoining husbands to cherish wives as they would their own bodies, while wives submit to husbands as the church submits to Christ.

Jesus, like Paul, identifies disciples or community members as siblings in a family focused on doing the will of the one heavenly Father. In Mark, Jesus prohibits divorce unequivocally, but in Matthew's gospel Jesus allows divorce under a single circumstance – adultery. In Matthew, certain disciples make themselves "eunuchs for the sake of the kingdom" as unmarried examples of single-minded devotion to God, an idea that is absent from the other gospels. Married disciples in Matthew, Mark and Luke profess to have left wives, families, professions and households to follow Jesus. In some passages, Jesus commands his would-be followers to repudiate family, wealth and property for the sake of the kingdom; in others, he commands individuals to return to family and community.

Paul's letters describe women like Phoebe as leaders of communities and heads of households. Households were not private and secluded as they might be today, but rather public and accessible to strangers. Heads of households, no matter how small, would have been responsible for slaves. Households then as now included relatives; in the gospels, Luke describes a household of five: father, son, mother, daughter, and mother-in-law.

Modern households might include children and ageing parents, grandchildren and grandparents, and children alongside grandchildren. As for Jesus' own family of origin, gospel writers never speak of Joseph as Jesus' father.

Women as disciples and models

Jesus was ahead of the curve in regard to single women. They were disciples, followers, conversation partners and friends. Jesus treated mothers as heads of households, married women as independent from their marriage and as single people. Women disciples and followers of Jesus included Mary Magdalene, Susanna, Joanna, and many others who provided economic support for Jesus' ministry.

Jesus' conversation partners included single parents like the Canaanite woman whose daughter Jesus healed, and married women like the woman at the well with whom Jesus preferred to dialogue as if she were single: "You are right in saying 'I have no husband' for you have had five husbands and he whom you now have is not your husband," Jesus tells her.

Jesus' itinerant ministry implies that female and male disciples must be willing and able to leave families of origin. Luke, the gospel writer who identifies wealthy and mobile female followers of Jesus, implies that Susanna was sufficiently affluent to make a financial contribution to the mission, sufficiently free of household responsibilities to accompany the mission and sufficiently healthy to serve.

Joanna is identified by her husband Chuza, a "steward" or a governor, overseer, or high-ranking administrator, with either economic or political authority in Herod's domain, attached to his private estate or appointed over a political district. Joanna is a continuing member of the mission, and is mentioned by name as a witness to the resurrection. Has she separated from Chuza? If Joanna follows the mission as a woman who has separated from her husband, then perhaps Luke is emphasizing the magnitude of personal sacrifice which disciples are willing to make; but then, where is Joanna getting the resources she is using to support the mission?

Independently wealthy women did exist in Jesus' world, but one of the socio-economic reasons for opposition to divorce was the destitution it often imposed on a divorced woman. Perhaps Joanna has not, in fact, separated from her husband, but has gone on mission with Chuza's permission or perhaps even under his direction. Luke may be implying that Chuza the steward of Herod approves of the mission sufficiently to be willing to second his wife to it and undergo the consequent deprivation.

A resurrected Jesus first appeared to a single woman, Mary Magdalene, according to John's gospel. She is commissioned to tell the other disciples what she has seen and heard.

Jesus' family values?

Family values are attributes and qualities affirmed socially and transmitted from one generation to another. Perhaps Jesus learned affirmation of women as independent followers, conversation partners, and friends from his mother. After all, she was an educated Jewish woman who almost became a single parent.

Thus the New Testament portrays a variety of ways in which the early believers became followers of Jesus in the differing circumstances of single, married, and community life. For us to isolate and commend one set of moral instructions over another fails to acknowledge the authority of the whole teaching. There is no unified teaching on marriage, divorce, households or families in the New Testament.

Since we can find implicit commendations of differing patterns of life – or, if you will, New Testament "lifestyles" – in various communities, it would seem imprudent to single out any one form of behaviour as authoritative. All must be regarded as provisional, since other models might rightfully also derive their authority from the New Testament. Furthermore, a multiplicity of community and personal life patterns is explicitly warranted by Paul's celebration of the diversity that constitutes the Body of Christ. Similarly, the authority of the Gospel is self-limiting and self-defining through the very fact that the church has canonised four distinct, often irreconcilably different, and equally authoritative Gospel witnesses.

It is very important to pay attention to the sociological and literary contexts of the gospels and Paul's letters. To understand Jesus' own household, the so-called "Holy Family" of Matthew's gospel, or the extended family of Luke, or the households from which disciples come, we need to take the contours of Roman households into account: husbands, wives, children, extended family members, slaves, and adopted children could and did characterise middle-sized households in outlying places of the empire, including Galilee. Family members also belonged to guilds in which members called each other "brothers." Literary context, on the other hand, shapes meaning and helps to interpret passages in light of a whole text.

When we hear readings from the Old Testament, the epistles or the gospels, we are encountering only isolated fragments of a larger whole. It is important to know that the version of the Lord's Prayer closest to the one we say in worship today occurs in the heart of the Sermon on the Mount, the first extended teaching of Jesus in Matthew's gospel. Jesus teaches the disciples (and others who may have heard the sermon) a concise prayer, the praying of which brings the community of the Heavenly Father into being. Similarly, today we say the Lord's Prayer together in the Eucharist just at the point before we receive communion. As part of the community of the Heavenly Father we say the Lord's Prayer together, petitioning God for the bread that sustains our lives.

We may also visualise a literary description through art. An icon or painting called "The Holy Family in Egypt," depicting Joseph, Mary and the infant Jesus in Mary's arms, may look like any husband, wife and child. I know it is Matthew because they are in Egypt, and so I can "read" this picture as a representation of Matthew's description of Joseph taking "the child and his mother" in and out of Egypt. In Matthew, Joseph is not the father of the child. The family may be holy, but it is not a husband, wife, and their child. Christian tradition has understood Matthew's wording to imply a distance between Joseph on the one hand and "the child and his mother" on the other. Thus, even if Joseph, Mary and her child look like a family unit, deeper investigation reveals that a closer analogy to the Holy Family may be to a family in which the child is born of the mother with an adoptive father.

By contrast, depictions of the Holy Family in Luke do not locate the "family" in Egypt but portray the infant Jesus with an older child, John, and his mother Elizabeth. Luke's accounts of the births of John the Baptist and Jesus focus on the relationship of the cousins, Elizabeth and Mary, and their miraculous births; they include characters like Elizabeth and Zechariah, Anna and Simeon, who appear nowhere else in the New Testament. Luke's notion of an extended family is of a piece with his larger vocabulary for houses and households, including terms for inns and innkeepers, the verb "to receive as a guest," and descriptions of a household that would terrify most of us: father, mother, son, daughter, and daughter's mother-in-law. Luke describes large houses with domestic and outdoor servants, medium houses with a few slaves, and poorer houses without slaves of any kind.

Reading ancient texts like the gospels or letters of Paul is hard work. It's not just a question of investigating ancient sociological or literary contexts; it's a question of asking critical questions about bringing ancient texts to bear on modern realities. Our interrogation of ancient texts, more often than not, lays bare not so much the texts as our own presuppositions. But our fidelity to these texts and their authority for us makes it imperative that we continue to do it in full awareness of the provisional character of our readings and applications.

Creativity, generosity and magnanimity

What does this look like in practice for twenty-first century Christians? If it looks like irreconcilably different worshippers gathered around the table of the Last Supper and celebrating salvation by Jesus Christ in vastly divergent patterns of life, is that not entirely congruent with the multiple witnesses presented in Scripture? Can we consciously and as a matter of policy exclude any member of the Body of Christ without damaging the whole? When I kneel side by side with someone whose construction of family looks radically different from mine, I witness to a God whose ways are not our ways, whose judgments cannot be limited by our finite understanding, whose generosity and creativity must not be circumscribed by our tiny hearts and minds.

Our decision to include all forms of family in the community of God may be misguided. Some configurations of family may be tares in the wheat of God's kingdom. But if, as Gamaliel said in Acts 5:38, "this plan or this undertaking is of human origin it will fail; but if it is of God, you will not be able to overthrow them." If we condemn, we contravene God's own commandments. The sure knowledge we have is that if we err on the side of generosity and magnanimity, we do not stray far from the nature of God, and we have a sure claim on God's forgiveness.

Notes

1. A good proportion of this chapter is excerpted from Deirdre Good, Jesus' Family Values (Church Publishing Inc., New York, NY, USA: 2007). Available in the UK via: http://books.ekklesia. co.uk/product_info.php?products_id=1951

2. Thanks for additional material go to Episcopal Café: http:// www.episcopalcafe.com/

Chapter Nine

Sexuality as an ecumenical challenge

Simon Barrow

'God's revelation in Christ is revelation in concealment, secrecy. All other so-called revelation is revelation in openness. But who then can see the revelation in concealment? .. Nobody [but those who see] God's judgement and grace in the midst of human weakness, sin and death, where otherwise [humanity] can see only godlessness.' – Dietrich Bonhoeffer, *The Theology of Crisis*

'To determine whether someone is truly religious we should observe not how they speak of God, but how they speak of the world.' – Simone Weil, *Gravity and Grace*

A journey of un-knowing

There are few subjects more exciting than human sexual activity or more potentially boring than ecumenical debate! So before I make a further small contribution to the Christian church's current over-excitability about sex, I need to offer an explanation for my consciously curious decision to approach it via ecumenism, of all things. As I do so, I hope you will come to agree with me that a substantial Christian contribution to our understanding of sexuality should be distinguishable primarily by its ability to make what we thought was plain less and less obvious. This, after all, according to no less an authority than St Paul (or, at least, a close associate of his) is precisely what the Easter Gospel is about — truth that demands much more than that which appears on the surface. For as we read in Colossians, 'the life you have is hidden with Christ in God.' [1]

I hope that we can therefore accept the shared role of being seekers rather than knowers on this subject – a theme on which many of Jesus' parables are premised. This quest for a 'new mind' on abiding concerns is also the reason why I have chosen not to pursue the more predictable route of addressing the question of the treatment of lesbian and gay people in the church through an examination of the recent state of ecumenical debate. That is well documented elsewhere and if I were to rehearse it I would simply be repeating well-worn arguments. [2] Instead I wish to suggest a different pattern of Christian engagement with the whole matter of human sexuality based on some larger ecumenical impulses.

So why ecumenism as the appropriate context for re-covering (or should I say 'un-knowing'?) human sexuality? [3] Most people, I would guess, think of ecumenism – if they think of it at all – as a strange but worthy activity practised by a few local enthusiasts who insist on making our Christian denominations do, from time-to-time, what they patently do not wish to do most of the time: recognise each other as a gift of God, and collaborate in ministry and mission. Alternatively, perhaps they (we?) think of ecumenical work primarily as a bureaucratic task of engineering doctrinal and functional agreement among the great confessions; or as a repository for strange and obscure bodies like the World Council of Churches or Churches Together in Britain and Ireland. [4] Either way, it's frankly not very sexy.

From church to kingdom

We can be thankful, then, that these activities and structures (useful though they may be) are not the main point of ecumenism. The Greek word from which get our term ecumenical, *oikumene*, is normally translated in a way which, curiously enough for something describing the historical movement which seeks a world alliance among Christians, does not start with the concept of 'church' at all. Rather, as you probably know, *oikos* means house or household, and mene comes from the verb 'to inhabit'. And so the word *oikumene*, which also has close associations with *oikonomia* (economy, the management of the household) first and foremost designates 'the whole inhabited earth' as the subject and locus of God's loving and saving activity.

This, of course, as the famous missionary conference in

Edinburgh 1910 which gave impetus to the modern ecumenical movement rightly understood, involves a key role for the church – but as servant rather than a master. On that latter point, Edinburgh (with the assumptions behind its call to 'evangelise the world in this generation') was perhaps less clear. But history has been wise in teaching Christians humility, the twentieth century particularly so. For the universal church of Jesus Christ, with all its historical glories and ignominies, its triumphs and tragedies, remains a signpost and a sacrament of something much more important than itself: the kingdom (or commonwealth) of God; that mysterious new creation for which Christ lived, died and was raised. [5]

Understood ecumenically, therefore, and stripped of its in-built tendencies to exercise mastery in the name of God, the church as the exemplary Body of Christ is called to be both a pointer to the power, presence and purpose of God for all things, and (though it may fall painfully short of this) 'God's experimental plot in human history.' [6]

Maybe that seems obvious enough to you, but I would contend that for all practical purposes it has been forgotten. It is overlooked both in the way that we as Christians live in the world generally, but also quite specifically by the way in which we as church fail to cope with the terrifying intimacies, joys and confusions of human sexuality – that dimension of ourselves by which we are most known and un-known.

It is in this fractured ecclesial context that I want to point up some of the key features of 'being ecumenical' which, I think, offer real hope and promise for moving beyond the current impasse which effects much of the church in its dealings with sexuality, and especially in its awkward (even oppressive) relationships with those whose gender, orientation or sexual identity is not as some say it 'should be'.

In identifying these features I am making the claim, of course, that ecumenism is not just some peculiar habit or a mere reflex of a group of hobbyists within our Christian traditions. Rather, it is the requirement continually to re-read those traditions in the light of the promise of the universal church and its message of hope.

The goal of communion

So, firstly, to be church ecumenically, as I have already implied, is to have faith in God's purposes for the whole world, not to be preoccupied with our role and status in helping to fulfil them. What are those purposes? In detail, we do not know. They are hidden, as St Matthew tells us, in the foundations of the world. [7] If we had to choose one word to characterise the emergence of this hidden purpose, however, I would suggest that it should be communion – the co-existence of all in God, and God in all. This, in its sacramental anticipation, is the very thing which most divides the churches, of course. Put that down to a combination of Christian fallibility and God's perverse sense of humour. But it still expresses, as no other word does, a hope for our universe which concerns the difficult possibility of relationship in the midst of destruction and division, of gift in the midst of greed and possession.

Communion (shrouded in mystery, like all the gifts of God) is therefore about the ways and means by which that which is disparate, different and potentially at odds can come into harmony. It is achieved not by the imposition of uniformity or domination – those are the ways of the world – but by the spirit of co-operative difference and willed good (goodwill). Think of the image of the Body of Christ: it paradoxically depends for its unity on collaborative difference, and also on a common mind which wills a place of honour for all, and most especially for those parts of the body which are sometimes marginalised or dishonoured. [8] It is for this possibility arising out of the scars of sin that Christ endured humiliation and public execution.

All this may seem a little abstract. If so, I apologise. I tend to think in theories. Jesus, more helpfully, preferred to picture the divine communion by telling stories about accursed Samaritans who broke religious taboos for the sake of good, prodigal offspring who discovered the quite contagious irresponsibility of unbounded love, women who found lost coins (probably under the noses of male accountants), prostitutes who were closer to God's kingdom than the righteous, and so on. All this, and much more that he said and did, is God's work, and it ought to be the work of the church too; though it usually isn't.

Now take a few moments to begin to think comparatively about the implications of all this for our understanding of human sexuality. Difference is what creates unity. What is considered dishonourable can be most honourable. Outsiders can be insiders. Everything that we are and can be may be woven into the fabric of God's gift; and, on the other hand, it can also become part of the hell which many of us create or participate in much of the time.

Therein lies not just the promise bound up with the nature of sexuality, but the judgement which that promise also brings. For the grace of God which invites us to build communion with those we are inclined to reject is not some 'woolly liberal' evasion, it is deeply radical and demanding. It is, to adapt Bonhoeffer's words, a gift which is free but costly. It requires immense courage and discipline to put our very selves (including our sexual selves) at the service of an ethic, an ethos, a movement towards wider community. Not only does it make it necessary for us to break down all that excludes and degrades human beings (be that the fearful homophobia of much of the church, or the depersonalising hedonism of much of the straight and QLGBT scenes); it also requires us to begin to live an alternative to those patterns of unjust discrimination which the church often inherits from the surrounding culture and then 'baptises' into its own way of being. [9] Of such challenges is the way of the Cross composed.

Now these are but glimpses of a different future for the church, but I hope they are sufficient to show that the truly ecumenical focus on God's action towards the communion of the whole world gives us an infinitely deeper, richer (and, frankly, more uncomfortable) palate to paint with than a few verses of Scripture torn from their context in the struggles of our forbears in faith to receive and live the message of God.

Custodians of the gift

This brings us, naturally enough, to the matter of the Bible. How does a church that recognises its ecumenical calling to live in communion with the past, present and future (the meaning of its universality) handle the sacred texts and traditions which represent the deposit of the faith of Christ received and transmitted in word and deed? For it is here in our founding texts that we contend most directly with revelation concealed, the eternal Word beckoning through the fallibility of flesh, the treasure hidden in clay pots.

Now I do not for one moment wish to engage in the game of the tribal interpretation of texts which characterises (and debases) so much of our current church 'debate' about sexuality. There is no future in that at all. What I want to do instead is to share two paradigmatic stories which offer hope for a new way in which the Word made words can once again be received as liberating gift, where usually it is turned into imprisoning ideology. This includes, especially, those elements of Scripture which appear most difficult to handle in the contemporary.

Some years ago, when I was working as an adult education adviser for the Church of England, I helped to lead a clergy retreat. One sunny day the assembled gathering was at Morning Prayer. The New Testament reading was a famous passage from Corinthians ('it is better to marry than to burn') which our lectionary delightfully decided to entitle 'Concerning Virgins'. [10] As we listened to St Paul's words there was some embarrassed giggling in the back pews. This was a sophisticated audience and they clearly found the rather extreme measures advocated by the Apostle a bit difficult to take. But this was Scripture, so we couldn't argue back. Could we? The person leading the intercessions was able to soothe the discomfort rather effectively in the circumstances. His concluding prayer went something along these lines: 'Lord, we have heard St Paul's confusion concerning virgins. We confess that we too are often confused in our sexuality and our relationships. Help us to discover your will in these things.' And so on. It seemed, as someone remarked afterwards, that this was the quintessential Anglican way to make 'the best of a bad job'! So we duly moved on and forgot about it.

The next day Bishop Peter Selby, who had been present throughout the retreat, was due to preach at the Eucharist. He announced that he had decided to begin by reflecting on this incident at Morning Prayer and its broader significance. He had imagined, he said, an encounter in heaven between St Paul and that person who had lead the intercessions the previous day. First of all, St Paul might begin by indicating how honoured he was to meet someone who saw through his confusions so readily! Secondly, and more seriously, the Apostle might say something like this: 'Of course, you were quite right. I was confused concerning virgins, and marriage in this instance, and homosexuality and much else when I wrote that letter. But there was one thing that I was not confused about. And that is what it means to have an undivided heart in the service of the kingdom of God.'

This strikes right to the core of the matter. For, as so often with biblical texts, both 'instinctive conservatives' and 'instinctive liberals' are apt to argue about the contested details and miss the central point. The key theological issue in 1 Corinthians 7 is not what we make of St Paul's culture-related assumptions about marriage and discipleship. For we may rightly conclude that life and understanding has moved on, and that we may not be wrong in handling these things differently today. But what we should never lose sight of is the controlling centre of his teaching: the need for 'an undivided heart' – that is, a way of living faithfully which does not divide off our relationships and our sexuality from our life in the presence of our fellow human beings and God, but which seeks instead an integration of all these things in the context of an inclusive community. Here is the kind of interpretative and responsive maturity which the multivalent biblical text demands of us as we face the challenges of the present.

The second example builds on this hermeneutical approach. In his inaugural address to the diocesan synod when he was translated to Worcester, the same bishop (who has been courageously open in his support of lesbian and gay people) took the opportunity to address the broader context for the debate in the Church of England on homosexuality and other matters of contention by looking at what a thoroughly radical engagement with Scripture and tradition might imply for us. He gave as one example the circumstances surrounding the Council of Jerusalem, recorded in Acts 15.

This, let us not forget, was the first ecumenical council of the church. It was an exercise in seeking the emergence of a communing Word through chaos and disagreement within the

Christian community about issues of fundamental identity -- namely the question of how to handle the differences over circumcision between Greek and Jewish Christians.

To us today, these disputes seem remote and even petty. But they are actually central to the Gospel. They concern the extent to which the Christian good news is subject to the constraints of tribe and race, and the matter of whether some religious practices are more a question of culture than of divine sanction, or vice versa.

The result of the Council of Jerusalem was, as Peter Selby reminded his audience, what many Christians today would call 'a fudge', and the minutes of the meeting are still in dispute! Nevertheless, the settlement attained helped the church to move forward in unity by refusing to elevate one group over the other. In so doing it created the conditions for a more inclusive (or should we say more anti-exclusive) understanding of the Gospel.

So even when the details are messy, the trajectory of the liberating and unconstrained love of God goes on generating the conditions for renewal – provided that we as church are prepared to take the risks involved. This entails recognising that faithfulness to an 'unchanging' Gospel may in fact demand radical change, because the world in which it has to be continually received never stands still. (Not to move in a shifting context is not to stay the same, but to lose ground.)

All this suggests to me a fluid but rigorous way of handling our texts, our traditions and our differences that moves beyond the arena of party dispute and forces us to ask the bigger questions: who is the Gospel for, a privileged few or the many? What difference does baptism make to our received customs, rituals and taboos? How can we develop an ethic for all (rather than an ethos of the presently powerful)? Above all, what does it mean, in the area of human sexuality, to have an undivided heart?

Moving towards 'the other' in Christ

A third key sign of a church which recognises itself to be ecumenical is that it seeks to be true to its origins as a Gospel movement which means, in particular, a movement that recognises the will of God for the whole inhabited earth as something that is especially disclosed by those who are marginal, oppressed and 'other'. This is what makes the ecumenical church a missionary church. Mission being, as the late South African theologian David Bosch once memorably noted, 'the church crossing frontiers in the guise of a servant' (Christ who remains present but hidden in our midst). [11]

Whatever its many woes, one of the greatest gains of the formal ecumenical movement over the course of this century has been its difficult but powerful discovery that, if we are to take the Gospel seriously, the first must be last, the rejected ones chosen, the poor exalted and the mighty thrown low for the good of all, and so that all may truly share. Communion again. But the metanoia, about-turning, which the following of Jesus Christ involves is not just a reversal of power (though it is certainly that), it is also and inescapably a transformation of the human heart.

So, for example, the economic reversal affected by the tax collector, Zaccheus, depended on a new estimation of what and who was valuable (one different to the value inscribed in the currency he so effectively manipulated). And the active goodness of that Good Samaritan depended upon him seeing a stranger as a brother, rather than as a sworn enemy. In this way alone was a new society made possible. Indeed, Jesus spoke openly of such a society in the Beatitudes as recorded in Matthew 5. Here he pictured a disparate, anti-exclusive group of people made up of those deprived of land, food and dignity, and of those who struggle with them – a community of the dispossessed who expressed the core of God's purposes in the world.

Again, this fundamental truth of the churches' calling to be a 'new society' has staggering implications for the way we see, experience and handle human sexuality. When the Gospel takes root strangers become companions, enemies become friends, and those who we castigate as 'others' (as 'unclean', perhaps) come to be seen as other selves, and remind us both of our own internal 'other' (that hidden part of ourselves which we ignore at our peril) and of the Other who we know, mysteriously and terrifyingly, as the Living God. A true conversion has occurred. And on this basis we can begin to deal with the public secret, the concealed revelation of ourselves which we call our sexuality. For just as we are hidden with Christ in God, so is our deepest identity, not least our sexual identity. But, as with the Gospel, it is hidden not just in isolated individuals, but in persons who are (fundamentally and inescapably) in relation. People in communion, or striving for it, or defacing it, or running away from it. [12]

Transforming our church ethos

To realise this need to encounter otherness as a relational gift of God is to begin to make sense of those identity, security and ethical questions which lie at the heart of the sexual agenda. Otherwise we end up in one of two untenable positions (if I may use such a term!) The first is a self-righteous moral conservatism which wields texts as weapons, seeking to replace spirit with law and God's open future with our unchanging past. The second is a gratuitous libertinism which mistakes license for freedom and gratification for fulfilment. What we need instead is an ethos, a way of relating in the light of the hope and promise of communion, which is infinitely more radical and demanding than either of those options. This ethos will be one that treats the confusions of human sexuality with reverence rather than disdain and honesty rather than avoidance. It will be an ethic which is most concerned with the quality and faithfulness of our human relationships, and is therefore perhaps a little less preoccupied with policing the form they take. [13]

The conditions for at least partially (but never fully) recovering such a kingdom-oriented ethos for the fulfilment of our diverse human sexualities are also both thoroughly ecumenical in shape. The first is the abandonment of the naturalistic fallacy which lies at the heart of much Christian moralising about sex: namely the inflexible belief in an unchanging natural order. ('Homosexuality is against creation,' I have heard it said.) This belief fails to recognise what any ecumenical church should know, which is that our destiny, being God-given, lies ahead of us. We are an eschatological people, and therefore a right understanding of our genesis is that (unlike the Christ of God) we are made, not begotten. We are who we are, but much more we are who we shall be: the perfected image of God. And by 'perfected' I mean, speaking from where we are right now, 'open to new possibility' as well as 'open to completion'. [14]

The second condition is that we recognise that salvation (wholeness) is to be experienced now or not at all. This is what it means for God's purposes to be concerned with the oikumene. Not that the fulfilment of the divine purpose is found here alone, but that its mysterious substance is felt fully in the midst of life – through those archetypal human activities of loving and working which Dorothee Soelle reminds us are the core of our adult experience. [15] Only when that is so does the Gospel for our boundary experiences (birth and death) make proper sense. It is all or nothing – and the all must be received here, not in some Platonic world of pure ideal abstracted from the fabric of actual living.

Again, this makes the matter of rethinking human sexuality theologically for a changing world a core Gospel issue — not a kind of awkward side-show, which is how some church leaders are apt to see it when unduly discomforted by the voices of those (lesbian and gay people) who they would somehow like to go away. [16]

So there you have it, an ecumenical vision within which we might hope to recover human sexuality beyond the current ecclesiastical 'trench warfare'. [17] One which takes universality, humility, service, movement, marginality, temporality, the surprising workings of the Holy Spirit and hope in God's open future as its defining characteristics. It leaves all the precise moral definitions undefined, all the hard pragmatic tasks still to be done, and its means of revelation is characteristically through concealment – the continuous, collective search for our place in the hiddeness of God's unsurpassable love. But I believe that it is only this kind of breadth of perspective, this scale of community and this persistence of hope that will provide the resources for us to find a better way forward. And if this makes us less clear and confident about what is 'right' and 'wrong' with other peoples' sexuality, well maybe that is something which God is quite deliberately asking us to live with.

An epilogue on the ecumenism of siblings

I should like to conclude with a very wise Jewish story [18] that neatly encapsulates what is involved in the way we handle human sexuality, sexual difference (and much else besides) as people of faith:

A rabbi once asked his disciples how one decided at what hour the night was over and the day had begun.

'It is perhaps when, from a distance, one can recognise the difference between a cow and a pig?' asked one of the disciples.

'No,' came the answer.

'It is perhaps when, from a distance, one can recognise the difference between a black and a white dog?'

'No,' the rabbi replied.

'But how can one decide?' asked one impatient disciple.

The rabbi responded: 'It is when one looks into another person's face and one can see one's brother or sister. Until then, the night is still with us and it is still dark.'

Notes

This is an amended version of an address given to a primarily Anglican church audience in Brighton in April 1998, in memory of my late father, Leslie Padday-Barrow. It was published as a booklet by Coleman Press in 1999, under the title 'Towards Communion: Recovering human sexuality as an ecumenical concern' and subsequently made available through my website: http://www. simonbarrow.net. It has only been very lightly edited, as I felt it was better to retain the ethos of the original.

1. See Colossians 3.3. The reference is to baptism as a death to old ways and old thoughts.

2. Many of the key perspectives and arguments are summarised in 'Homosexuality: Some elements for an ecumenical discussion', The Ecumenical Review, Volume 50, No 1, January 1998. See: http://

*findarticles.com/p/articles/mi_m2065/is_n1_v50/ai_20344100/pg_
1, accessed 2 May 2008.*

*3. I am taking it as read here that genuine learning involves
a degree of un-learning (or 'un-knowing'), which in turn implies
that the 'learner' or 'knower' is willing to be disturbed. This is
a largely absent feature of ecclesiastical discussions concerning
human sexuality, as Savi Hensman points out elsewhere in this
collection. It is one which needs urgently to be reinstated.*

*4. Since 1990 the British and Irish ecumenical instruments
set up through the Not Strangers but Pilgrims process have
attempted a different model to the traditional ways of what we
might term 'activist' and 'institutional' ecumenism. This is the
'churches together' approach. It has been beneficial in encouraging
collaboration in some areas of church life, but not so far in those
(such as human sexuality) where the disagreements within and
between denominations run deepest.*

*5. The word 'kingdom' is the one most used for the coming new
reality which God is bringing about. I prefer 'commonwealth' or
kin-dom', because it captures the flavour of 'God's domination-free
order' (Walter Wink) much better than the traditional, hierarchical
and patriarchal language. It is therefore, I believe, much closer to
the preaching of Jesus.*

*6. The phrase is that of the Mennonite theologian John Driver,
from his book Images of the Church in Mission (Herald Press,
1997).*

7. St Matthew 13.35.

8. 1 Corinthians 12 and elsewhere.

*9. I am not using the term 'homophobia' to demonise those who
oppose equal rights for homosexual persons in church and society.
It is a term which refers to a deep seated fear of homosexuality (not*

necessarily lesbian and gay people per se), and it is very much connected with heterophobia in my view – about which, see note 17.

10. See I Corinthians 7.

11. This phrase was coined, I believe, in one of the late David Bosch's less known works, A Spirituality of the Road (Herald Press, 1983).

12. This argument is also developed in my article 'Encountering otherness in Christ', Christian magazine, Passiontide 1998.

13. On this question, see Sue Walrond-Skinner, The Fulcrum and the Fire (Darton, Longman and Todd, 1995).

14. This is the framework within which we can begin to understand St Paul's difficulties in Romans 1. See also James Alison's remarkable article, 'But the Bible says...'? A Catholic reading of Romans 1 (2007) – http://www.jamesalison.co.uk/texts/eng15.html

15. Dorothee Soelle & Shirley A Cloyes, To Work and to Love: Towards a theology of creation (Fortress, 1987).

16. Those who wish to explore the debates in the churches more fully should consult Elizabeth Stuart and Adrian Thatcher (Eds.), What the churches teach about sex (Mowbray, 1997).

17. I am well aware that the theological perspective I am offering here will not immediately be seen as a way forward by those within the church who are making a narrow approach to human sexuality a 'defining issue' for quite different reasons. But what we have to do with them, I believe, is to refocus the debate onto the question of what is centrally at stake in the Gospel. This is one of the things that helped change people's minds on the question of slavery, which was widely held to be 'biblical' in earlier times.

For it is a tribal misconstrual of the Christian message based on heterophobia (fear of the other) which I believe lies at the heart of much anti-gay sentiment. That and a (rightful) concern that we should not change the understanding of the church on grounds other than solidly theological ones.

18. Quoted in The Ecumenical Review, Volume 50, No 1, January 1998.

Part Four: Learning

Chapter Ten

In search of textual healing

Christopher Rowland

Less than 20 years after the death of Jesus, Jews and pagans in a city in Syria were eating together on a regular basis. Jews relaxed the rules which had hitherto maintained their identity. Experience of God, and of each other, led those men and women to new patterns of behaviour.

Paul describes the behaviour of those Christians in Antioch in his Letter to the Galatians, when he stood up in defence of them to his fellow church leaders, who had suddenly got cold feet about their participation in this kind of practice.

Not surprisingly such activity caused scandal among more conservative elements in the church. Representations were sent from Jerusalem asking Paul, and these newly established communities, to desist from this unscriptural behaviour. Standing up to those who did not want to rock the boat was crucial for Paul, as something important about the gospel was in danger of being sacrificed.

Paul had little or no basis in scripture for his decision to support this kind of mixed dining and shared fellowship. Indeed, his opponents had all the best arguments from precedent and scripture on their side. Nevertheless, he was persuaded that the experience of God of those pagans, who had converted to Christ, corresponded to what he, and other Jewish Christians, had experienced, and was an authentic mark of God's presence.

There is a similar reaction on Peter's part in Acts, when he was persuaded, as a result of his dream and the conversion of the Roman centurion Cornelius, that the same God was at work in these pagan converts as had been at work in the first Christians. So he asserts, "God gave the pagans the same gift as us when we believed; who was I to hinder God?"

The world turned upside-down

What both Peter and Paul were doing was rejecting precedent and tradition in the light of experience. They read scripture in a way that was determined by the experience of the love of Christ and the obvious marks of God's presence in the lives of those who, according to the law, should be outsiders. In so doing, they laid down an approach to reading the Bible which should be central to Christianity.

Thanks to Paul, Christianity has never really been a religion that used the Bible as a code of law. In his Second Letter to the Corinthians, he writes: "The letter kills, the Spirit gives life." Throughout his writings, he tries to get at what the Bible means, with the central criterion being conformity to Christ. He pioneered an approach to the Bible which also applies to his words in the New Testament. We should not concentrate on the letter of the text, but try to get at the underlying point of his words.

So, basing one's attitudes towards gay and lesbian people merely on two verses from Romans and Corinthians I, plus a handful of decontextualised verses from the Hebrew Scriptures, runs the risk of ending up with a form of religion which is based on the letter of the text – something Paul empathically opposes – rather than on what a loving God is doing in transforming lives in the present.

On the Damascus road, Saul's world was turned upside down. He encountered Christ in the outsiders, the heretics, the misfits and aliens, the very people whom he had been commissioned to round up. It was this experience that transformed his life. Such a turnaround was not the result of minute attention to text and precedent.

The era of Paul and the early church was a time of experimentation as to what it meant to be God's people. As such, it may be particularly apposite for our time. When Canon Jeffrey John had to step down from the appointment to the Bishopric of Oxford in 2003 because of his long-term partnership, it was, for many of us, our "Antioch incident", when a stand has to be taken to bear witness to that which is true - our experience of God.

The appeal to precedent and tradition may have to be jettisoned in favour of the recognition that the same gift is at work in gay and lesbian Christians as in heterosexual Christians, and that the God who called Paul to explore new patterns of relationship is at work in committed same-sex relationships.

Note

This article first appeared in the Guardian newspaper as a Face to Faith column, and then on Ekklesia. It is reproduced with grateful acknowledgement.

Chapter Eleven

Listening and learning scripturally

Savitri Hensman

Current debates among Christians, especially on human sexuality, often focus on how the Bible should be read. Some of the people who regard themselves as 'Bible-believing' resist the idea that they might gain much from listening and dialogue, observation and study. From their point of view, the truth has been revealed in Scripture, and this is decisive. However there are other people who believe that Christians should be open to advances in knowledge and what the Holy Spirit might be revealing in today's world. Some play down the relevance of much of the Bible except as a source of doctrine about God.

Yet the Bible itself seems, to some readers, to point to the vital importance of being attentive to the wider world and people's experiences. The Gospel accounts of the teaching and actions of Jesus Christ, in particular, may offer valuable insights on how contentious issues could be approached. Some of the relevant themes are explored below.

Giving a fair hearing

It is today widely accepted that, if those in authority are to make a decision which will profoundly affect certain people's lives, those people have a right to be heard. If, for instance, a court's decision might result in someone losing his livelihood or liberty, it would be regarded as unjust if that person were not given an opportunity to argue his case with the aid of a competent lawyer, bring evidence and respond to accusations. And it would be regarded as unjust for a state agency to build a road through someone's land unless she had been given the chance to put her own view forward and this had been properly considered. Being judged without being heard can undermine people's sense of personhood, and those such as dictators and brutal jailers who wish to break the spirit of those in their charge may make use of this.

The right to a fair hearing is not a new principle. The Old Testament emphasises its importance: 'You must not be partial in judging: hear out the small and the great alike', Moses urges the judges he has appointed (Deuteronomy 1.17). Yet this is a world where, all too often, bitter rivalry and injustice are encountered, where 'each hunts the other with a net', 'the prince and the judge ask for a bribe' (Micah 7.2-3) and wicked rulers 'condemn the innocent to death' (Psalm 94.20-21) Even those who are usually just may be led astray, though listening may set them back on the right path; David is so enraged by the rude inhospitality of a rich livestock farmer, Nabal, that a bloodbath almost follows, until his wife Abigail rushes out to plead with the young warrior. David listens, and afterwards is profoundly grateful: 'Blessed be the Lord, the God of Israel, who sent you this day to meet me! Blessed be your discretion, and blessed be you, who have kept me this day from bloodguilt and from avenging myself with my own hand!' (1 Samuel 25.2-35).

In the New Testament, too, those in positions of responsibility are required at least to try to be just, while God goes beyond mere justice and is more merciful than people deserve or expect. The seemingly powerless move out of the margins and find a voice. Indeed, the hero of one of Jesus' parables in Luke's Gospel is a widow who is so persistent that she manages to get a judge who has 'no fear of God and no respect for anyone' to listen to her demand for justice and take action! (Luke 18.1-8).

It is of course courteous for people in general to listen to one another, but there is a particular obligation for those in positions of power. A judge's feelings may be hurt if a defendant is rude to him, but the defendant's life may be shattered if the judge refuses to allow evidence which would prove her innocent. Making every effort to allow different perspectives to be heard is all the more important because it is all too easy to hear only what fits in with one's preconceived notions and filter out anything else.

Church leaders in today's world exercise power within Christian communities, and often considerable influence in society, and part of their vocation is to listen with attentiveness and humility not only to ecclesiastical superiors and wealthy patrons but also the poor and marginalised. This can be hard. People in congregations and dioceses are often deferential and avoid challenging what leaders say, and it can be tempting for them to come to believe they can make pronouncements on those with less power without making an effort to hear their perspective. For instance male clerics may feel they can offer guidance on how women should behave without hearing from women, other than those who submit to their own authority and echo their own views. And lay and clerical leaders who are reasonably well-off by the standards of their communities may pronounce on economic issues without studying these in depth or listening to various perspectives from poor people.

All too often, lesbian, gay and bisexual people are talked about without being heard ourselves, and our families and friends may also go unheard. For instance, church leaders who have never knowingly spent time with same-sex couples, and whose lesbian and gay acquaintances are generally closeted and unwilling to speak honestly for fear of being penalised by society or the church, may make sweeping statements about same-sex relationships. This is unjust: all should be given a fair hearing on matters that affect their lives.

Avoiding 'false witness, slander'

In Matthew's and Mark's Gospels, when Jesus is challenging the notion of purity held by the religious leaders of his day, he discusses what makes someone unclean. 'Listen and understand: it is not what goes into the mouth that defiles a person, but it is what comes out of the mouth that defiles... what comes out of the mouth proceeds from the heart, and this is what defiles. For out of the heart come evil intentions... false witness, slander' (see Matthew 15.1-20; also Mark 7.1-23 in the New Revised Standard Version).

The wrongness of making negative statements about other people which are untrue is mentioned in various other Biblical passages, including the Ten Commandments (Exodus 20.16). This is perhaps because it is so easy for humans to do, for instance to gain an advantage, give vent to jealousy, pursue a grudge or go along with the prejudices of a particular social group. Such false claims may arise from deliberate malice or willingness to believe the worst of certain people without being open to evidence which may lead in a different direction. Instead of seeing each person as a unique child of God, she or he may be stereotyped as unclean, dishonest, useless or dangerous.

Negative rumours and prejudice can do considerable damage. James, in his Epistle, warns that 'every species of beast and bird, of reptile and sea creature, can be tamed and has been tamed by the human species, but no one can tame the tongue – a restless evil, full of deadly poison. With it we bless the Lord and Father, and with it we curse those who are made in the likeness of God. From the same mouth come blessing and cursing. My brothers and sisters, this ought not to be so. Does a spring pour forth from the same opening both fresh and brackish water?' (see James 3. 1-12).

People, families and communities can find themselves shunned or even attacked because of the bad things said about them. In many societies, for instance, particular ethnic groups can become targets. Worryingly, the Bible itself has been misused, for instance to justify discrimination and violence against Jewish people and women labelled as 'witches'. What was intended to edify and uplift may be twisted by the fear, prejudice or greed in human hearts into an excuse for maligning one's neighbour.

Lesbian, gay and bisexual people have often been at the receiving end of such vilification. Sometimes from an early age, perhaps before we can name our feelings which set us apart from the majority, we can find ourselves targeted on the basis of half-truths and untruths. This is not to claim that we are saintly victims: we are ourselves capable of prejudice against other minorities, and indeed against ourselves, turning hatred and contempt inwards.

It is sometimes claimed that our actions, and even our orientation, arises from wilful selfishness, despite all the evidence to the contrary. There is often a refusal to acknowledge that, especially in places where we can live together openly, many of our relationships embody faithful and long-lasting love and self-sacrifice, and mutual care for other family members and neighbours.

It is not only in wider society that we are reviled but even in church circles. On such an emotionally charged issue as human sexuality, 'deep and dispassionate study' which takes seriously 'Scripture and the results of scientific and medical research', and genuine 'dialogue' (to use the words of the 1978 Lambeth Conference), are much needed. Yet some of the language used by church leaders makes this difficult, for instance claims that homosexuals are 'deviants', that our behaviour is equivalent to bestiality and comes 'directly from the pit of hell'. Even such a carefully-worded document as the 1997 Kuala Lumpur Statement uses language in a way that can confuse rather than clarify when it states that 'The Holy Scriptures are clear in teaching that all sexual promiscuity is sin. We are convinced that this includes homosexual practices between men or women, as well as heterosexual relationships outside marriage.' However, whether or not partners entering a monogamous same-sex partnership are right or wrong to do so, they are not promiscuous in the usual sense of the word.

The false witness of some religious leaders has helped to create a climate which makes reasoned discussion difficult and in which some people feel justified in denying us basic human rights, even locking up, attacking or killing us. Our families and friends, too, may suffer. We may believe and internalise the negative images of us, and act accordingly. However, to those who know that such claims are untrue, it is the credibility of the church which may suffer. Why should those who make untrue statements about lesbians and gays be believed when they talk of the good news of Jesus Christ? So the ministry and mission of the Church are undermined.

Not 'straining out a gnat and swallowing a camel'

For everyone, keeping a sense of perspective is sometimes difficult. Self-interest, and the dominant views in one's own society, can all too often lead to exaggerated importance being given to some issues, and not enough emphasis to others. The vivid and comic picture painted in the Gospels by Jesus in his criticism of those who are judgmental – 'Why do you see the speck in your neighbour's eye, but do not notice the log in your own eye?' (see Matthew 7.1-5, Luke 6.37-42) – is still relevant.

Being knowledgeable and scrupulous about scriptural teachings does not necessarily ensure balance: Jesus also challenged the ultra-religious who 'tithe mint, dill, and cumin, and have neglected the weightier matters of the law: justice and mercy and faith', who 'strain out a gnat but swallow a camel!' (Matthew 23.23-24). Those so pious that they seek to abide by God's will in even the smallest things and encourage others to do the same can get their priorities wrong.

Sometimes those with a different perspective can play an important part in jolting humans into recognising what is most important and urgent. The authors of the book of Isaiah challenged the religious of their day, who asked why God did not respond to their piety: 'If you remove the yoke from among you, the pointing of the finger, the speaking of evil, if you offer your food to the hungry and satisfy the needs of the afflicted, then your light shall rise in the darkness and your gloom be like the noonday' (See Isaiah 58). True worship of God, who delights in generosity and mercy, does not involve oppressing and condemning others while neglecting the needy and vulnerable and upholding exploitative and violent social systems.

Time and again, the prophets challenge their listeners to question what they take for granted, as does Jesus in the Gospels. Throughout history, scholars and campaigners, and the voices of the downtrodden and marginalised themselves, have helped people to reassess what is most important. This is especially important on complex ethical matters or where there are competing priorities.

There is of course ongoing debate about human sexuality, and the circumstances in which physical intimacy is proper. This is important, but is it truly the central question for Christians today, and if so why? A handful of passages from the epistles, the meaning and in some cases translation of which is much disputed, are frequently quoted, but Paul is not preoccupied by sex. Romans 1, for instance, includes, 'For the wrath of God is revealed from heaven against all ungodliness and wickedness of those who by their wickedness suppress the truth.... They were filled with every kind of wickedness, evil, covetousness, malice. Full of envy, murder, strife, deceit, craftiness, they are gossips, slanderers...' Yet the spiritual dangers of malice and slander directed against minorities and people of lower social status are often overlooked, and the main point that Paul is trying to get across lost through too narrow a focus.

The priority which some Christians give to denouncing gay and lesbian partnerships, and the passion which this arouses, are disproportionate in a world where so many are starving, victims of war, enslaved or abused. Indeed homophobia and other forms of prejudice can be ways of avoiding the distress and uncertainty that some would otherwise feel amidst so much insecurity and suffering, and difficult questions about personal and collective responsibility. In today's world, as in ancient times, it is all too easy to 'strain out a gnat and swallow a camel'.

Loving one's neighbour as oneself

To 'love your neighbour as yourself' is indeed more important than burnt offerings and sacrifices (Mark 12.28-34, Matthew 22.36-40). But pious observance is in some ways easier. For some people, caring even for themselves is hard, but at least they are likely to know if they have a headache or if they feel like crying or laughing. They will also, unless they have severe memory problems, know something about their lives, for instance whom they rely on or who has threatened them.

Yet it may be difficult to understand the inner world of those who are close friends or relatives, let alone strangers and members of other communities. This may partly be because people sometimes avoid certain topics and hide their feelings, fearing that these are wrong or will cause them to be criticised or that others will be upset. Wives may not speak of their fears and frustrations to their husbands, laypeople may be polite and respectful to senior clergy but not reveal certain thoughts and experiences, young people becoming aware that they are attracted to members of the same sex may not mention this to their parents or peers. And those in leadership positions may lead busy lives, not having much time to listen except to those whose support or cooperation they need, and may feel so confident about their own knowledge that other people's fears and longings, joys and sorrows can go unnoticed.

This can make love difficult, unless it is a kind of impersonal charity or brisk kindness. Sometimes, indeed, needs and their solutions are obvious, but at other times this requires attentive listening. A good doctor will tend to listen carefully to his or her patients, to other caregivers who may have observed something the doctor has not and to researchers and others with useful knowledge about improving health, and be aware of the risk of making assumptions about the right course of action. A good friend, too, will tend to try to be open to what their companion is trying to tell them in words, gestures and silences, even if this may be uncomfortable. Job's friends would have been better off just keeping him company in his sorrow than coming up with seemingly pious comments which turned out, in the end, to be based on a misunderstanding of God's ways (Book of Job).

In the Gospel story of the rich man and Lazarus (Luke 16.19-31), there is no indication that the rich man is not religiously observant; indeed those who thrive while others suffer may be encouraged in their complacency by reading carefully-selected verses of Scripture (see, for example, Proverbs 3.9-10, 6.9-11). Yet he is barely aware of the reality of the beggar at his gate, and this distance from his neighbour distances him from God.

Christians often claim to 'love' everyone, but may be acting on their own unconscious wants and unexamined beliefs and be insensitive to others, especially those who are 'different' and marginalised. 'How does God's love abide in anyone who has the world's goods and sees a brother or sister in need and yet refuses help?' asks 1 John. 'Little children, let us love, not in word or speech, but in truth and action' (1 John 3.17-18). To lesbian, gay and bisexual people, claims to 'love' us by people who know little about our lives and seem unconcerned about the daily realities which confront us may appear hollow. If others truly listen to us, even if there are disagreements on some matters, we know that they are disagreeing with us, rather than some imagined version of us, and that this happens in the context of a love which can enable an ongoing relationship. And, in addressing our experiences, they may be enabled to recognise the often virulent homophobia which still infects all too many people, doing great spiritual harm to them as well as to us, and challenge it more effectively.

Being open to the Wisdom from above

The book of Proverbs recounts how Wisdom 'cries out in the street; in the squares she raises her voice', and emphasises the value of 'making your ear attentive to wisdom and inclining your heart to understanding', of searching for understanding 'as for hidden treasures' (see Proverbs 1.20-21, 2.1-7). Indeed this and several other books of the Bible are designated as 'wisdom' books, and Wisdom is central to some of the Deuterocanonical works. 'If you love to listen you will gain knowledge,' urges the book of Sirach, and 'Do not find fault before you investigate; examine first, and then criticise' (Sirach 6.33, 11.7).

The wise are not content simply to accept what is on the surface but will dig deeper. In the Deuterocanonical story of Susanna, judges are faced with what seems on the surface a straightforward case: two elders, men looked up to as guardians of morality in the community, have witnessed a young wife engaging in adultery. She denies it but, in a patriarchal set-up, her testimony carries far less weight than that of her accusers, who are themselves judges, and she is condemned. Young Daniel, however, inspired by God, challenges the verdict, asking his community whether they are really willing 'to condemn a daughter of Israel without examination and without learning the facts?' He probes the evidence for the prosecution – and it falls apart. In fact, the elders are seeking revenge because they have sexually harassed Susannah and she has not given way to them: it is they who at fault, yet without Daniel's intervention it is she who would have been punished (see Susanna).

Wisdom, whom some commentators identify with the Holy Spirit, also features prominently in the New Testament. For instance in the epistle to the Ephesians the author prays 'that the God of our Lord Jesus Christ, the Father of glory, may give you a spirit of wisdom and revelation as you come to know him' (Ephesians 1.17). 'Who is wise and understanding among you?' asks James. 'Show by your good life that your works are done with gentleness born of wisdom. But if you have bitter envy and selfish ambition in your hearts, do not be boastful and false to the truth. Such wisdom does not come down from above, but is earthly, unspiritual, devilish. For where there is envy and selfish ambition, there will also be disorder and wickedness of every kind. But the wisdom from above is first pure, then peaceable, gentle, willing to yield, full of mercy and good fruits, without a trace of partiality or hypocrisy. And a harvest of righteousness is sown in peace for those who make peace.' Wisdom from above leads to right relationship with God and neighbour.

In the parable in Luke's Gospel of the steward facing dismissal who fiddles the accounts to reduce the sums owed by his master's debtors, so that he has their goodwill to fall back on when he loses his job, his master praises him 'because he had done wisely: for the children of this world are in their generation wiser than the children of light'.1 This rings true even today: while salespersons may listen attentively to prospective clients and go to great lengths to strike up a rapport, Christians may be so wrapped up in piety that not enough loving attention is paid to feelings and needs of others. Yet in Matthew's Gospel, at the last judgement the righteous are told that 'just as you did it to one of the least of these who are members of my family, you did it to me' (Matthew 25.40).

Truly listening to lesbian, gay, bisexual and trans people, and studying material on sexuality by scholars from different disciplines and standpoints, may at first be uncomfortable for some Christians. It may involve dealing with matters of bodily intimacy and family life – subjects which may arouse strong emotions; coping with the challenge of taking on board unfamiliar experiences and re-examining long-held assumptions; and risking anger from church members who feel undermined or threatened, as well as the complications of church politics. This may involve an element of renunciation, even death to self, and yet beyond this lies the hope of resurrection into a life where those previously marginalised are now beloved brothers and sisters.

Following Jesus

Through Christ's example as well as teaching, readers of the Gospels can learn about the value – and difficulty – of offering the marginalised a chance to be heard, avoiding false witness and excessive harshness, loving one's neighbour as oneself and being open to divine wisdom.

Jesus is portrayed not as teaching and healing in an impersonal way but is wonderfully attentive to those around him, taking seriously those whom others would write off, ready to have detailed theological discussions not only with learned scholars but also with a Samaritan woman with a far-from-regular family life, to the surprise of his followers (John 4.1-2). Each person matters, and is different: when a woman with a haemorrhage touches him, even in the midst of the crowd he senses her and calls her out to tell her story, then praises her faith, so that one who was 'unclean' and destitute is heard by many and respected (Mark 5.24-34). When he is condemned by the pious for eating and drinking with tax collectors and sinners, he urges them, 'Go and learn what this means, "I desire mercy, not sacrifice"'(Matthew 9.10-13).

In Mark's gospel, it is understandable that his critics are appalled when he appears to be justifying defiance of God's own words, set out clearly in Scripture (Mark 2.23-28), with the claim that 'The sabbath was made for humankind, and not humankind for the sabbath.' What is more, he himself engages in sabbath-breaking (Mark 3.1-6), which they have been taught from childhood is a sin so grievous that the penalty is to be cut off from the community or even killed (Matthew 5.21-22).

The Sermon on the Mount in Matthew's gospel indicates that Jesus' understanding of the Old Testament is profoundly affected by his compassionate attentiveness to human need and deep awareness of the corrosive effects of anger and contempt. 'You have heard that it was said to those of ancient times, "You shall not murder": and "whoever murders shall be liable to judgement." But I say to you that of you are angry with a brother or sister, you will be liable to judgement; and if you insult a brother or sister, you will be liable to the council; and if you say, "You fool," you will be liable to the hell of fire (Matthew 5.21-22). (There has been much written about the precise meaning of the wording, including whether there is a direct reference to insults based on sexuality [Varnell – see endnote]. Certainly there is a glimmer of humour in the notion of being hauled in front of the Sanhedrin to explain to learned judges what is an everyday form of speech – but behind this is a serious warning that such attitudes can cause serious harm and even destroy lives.)

Anglicans have long tended to emphasise the value of Scripture, tradition and reason, and indeed these are closely intertwined. It is very difficult indeed to read a text without being in some way influenced by the expectations and desires of oneself and one's community, and unless one is aware of these tendencies, it is possible to be certain that the words have a particular meaning when, in fact, they could be understood in a different way. Those who mix mainly with the likeminded and do not listen to alternative perspectives may be reinforced in their view that theirs is the only true way. Tragically, in the gospels, many of those most passionately opposed to Jesus believe they are conscientiously obeying God's will as set out in Scripture: but in trying to show reverence for the words of God they unwittingly seek to kill God's living Word.

John's gospel portrays the dogmatic refusal of the religious authorities, who believe they are safeguarding God's law and tradition, to consider the possibility that this wandering preacher and healer, whom they believe is leading people astray, might be doing God's will (let alone God incarnate). When the police are so impressed by Jesus that they refuse to arrest him, the leaders ask, 'Surely you have not been deceived too, have you? Have any one of the authorities or of the Pharisees believed in him? But this crowd, who do not know the law – they are accursed.' And when dissident religious leader Nicodemus points out, 'Our law does not judge people without first giving them a hearing to find out what they are doing, does it?' his colleagues are dismissive (John 7.45-52). From their point of view, they know what Scripture and tradition teach, and must safeguard it. Christians who are honest would probably admit that church hierarchies can sometimes act like the Jewish authorities portrayed in the gospels, so wedded to the familiar that they fail to acknowledge what God is doing in their midst. And now, as in the past, humility and faith like that of Rabbi Gamaliel, who in the book of Acts opposes the persecution of the Christians (Acts 5.27-39), can be hard to sustain, especially when others are urging that what seems heretical must be stamped out.

Even today, religious leaders may refuse to consider the kind of evidence to which (in Matthew's and Luke's accounts) Jesus refers the followers of John the Baptist, sent to check whether he really is the saviour – 'Go and tell John what you hear and see' (Matthew 11.2-6, Luke 7.18-23), or which he cites when explaining how to distinguish between true and false prophets: 'A good tree cannot bear bad fruit, nor can a bad tree bear good fruit.'(Matthew 7.15-20, Luke 6.43-46). But many Christians know from experience that Scripture and tradition can yield unexpected treasures when read in the light of knowledge gained from painstaking study and hard-won experience.

In one scene is the gospels, Jesus expresses his frustration at the hardened hearts and closed minds of those who will not listen: 'The queen of the South will rise up at the judgement with this generation and condemn it, because she came from the ends of the earth to listen to the wisdom of Solomon, and see, something greater than Solomon is here!'(Matthew 12.42). One can imagine the indignation of pompous male religious leaders at being compared unfavourably with this foreign woman, whose beliefs and lifestyle were unlikely to have met with their approval! But the lengths to which she and others pursuing wisdom went are indeed impressive (1 Kings 4.29-34, 10.1-13).

Before the days of the printing press, film and internet, when so many instruments used in modern science had not been invented and investigative techniques now taken for granted had not been devised, gaining and sharing knowledge and deepening understanding could involve huge effort for what might seem like limited gains. It could be all too difficult to distinguish truth from myth, decide whether travellers' tales were factually based or tall stories and find out what treatments might work for sick people, yet there were some who made the effort. Today, it is easy for those who are literate – now a large proportion of the world's population – to read about the lives, hopes and fears of people living thousands of miles away, or watch documentary footage of creatures so tiny that they can barely be seen with the naked eye. There are fewer excuses for failing to seek in-depth knowledge and understanding, weighing up different perspectives and making informed decisions.

Christians in the twenty-first century can follow the example of the queen of Sheba without having to spend months in travelling across the globe!

However, as in the past, people tend to be reluctant to rethink their views, especially those on which they have acted – one reason that miscarriages of justice are so hard to correct even when evidence comes to light that shows the innocence of someone unjustly convicted of a crime. Tobacco companies may fund dubious 'research' which supposedly proves that cigarettes are not really that harmful, and some of their senior managers may themselves be smokers, despite all that is now known about the health hazards. Shying away from uncertainty and the possibility of change, especially where this may mean admitting to have harmed one's neighbour, is an aspect of human weakness to which both believers and unbelievers are prone. Indeed people of faith may project on to God their own misconceptions, claiming that their refusal to listen carefully and study diligently is a sign of how good and faithful they are. Yet, in the end, 'Wisdom is vindicated by her deeds', or in another version 'Wisdom is vindicated by all her children' (Matthew 11.19, Luke 7.35).

The story of the Syro-Phoenician woman, about which much has been written, is a particularly startling example of divine humility, and underlines the importance of listening. In Matthew's version (15.21-28), Jesus, who is uniquely close to the Father, is at first clear about his mission: he has been sent to the Jewish people. This makes sense: if he can win over those most likely to be receptive to the proclamation of the Kingdom of Heaven, they can go out and make disciples of all nations (Isaiah 55.3-5, 56.3-8); but if he gets deflected, the whole enterprise may fail. Who would know best what the Father wills, the beloved Son or a woman whose community's beliefs distort what is sacred, and who perhaps engages in unsavoury religious practices herself? What point is there in listening? Yet Jesus listens, debates with her, recognises wisdom in her response – and does what she asks! If Jesus is depicted in the gospels as showing such openness, perhaps it is not beneath the dignity of church leaders today to do likewise, and Wisdom may bestow unexpected treasures on them and those around them.

Moving forward on the listening process

While a process of study and dialogue on human sexuality has supposedly been going on for thirty years or so across the Anglican Communion, in some provinces this has been hampered by various factors, including the urgency of other problems and repressive attitudes from state and society which make it dangerous for lesbian, gay, bisexual and transgendered people and their family members to talk too openly about their experience. Even journalists and academics may decide, in such circumstances, not to go too deeply into the issues, and deliberately or unwittingly they may pass on half-truths or untruths.

Nevertheless, even in the midst of the harshest circumstances, including sometimes enforced secrecy, many QLGBT people have managed to live with some measure of dignity and develop loving and self-sacrificing relationships with partners, other relatives and friends and those in need in their communities. Some are now in their latter years, and able to look back and reflect on the often unexpected twists and turns that their lives have taken, perhaps discerning God's faithful love at work even in the midst of turmoil and uncertainty. There are also many local Christian communities whose members have struggled with questions of human sexuality over the years, watching sons and daughters, nieces and nephews, godchildren, babies they have baptised and children they have taught in Sunday school grow up and discover that they are lesbian, gay, bisexual or transgendered. Many have come to understand things in a different light. Their testimony too should be heard.

One of the greatest obstacles however is the all-too-common notion that one must choose between being 'Bible-believing' or taking people's experience seriously. Yet many of the authors of the books which came to be included in the Bible, while obviously not having access to all aspects of modern knowledge, were perhaps more sophisticated in their approach than some Christians today. These writers understood that the Scripture could take on different meanings, harmful or liberating, depending on the extent to which readers were open to God and compassionately attentive to their neighbours. Time and again, they underlined the importance of listening carefully and seeking truth, however uncomfortable or seemingly strange. Even now, members of the church may find that, in listening to strangers or outsiders who contradict what others take for granted, it is possible to be refreshed by the good news, (Mark 6.7-13) or even to encounter the living God (Luke 24.13-32).

Notes

1. As part of the 'listening process' in the Anglican Communion over the extensive disagreements about human sexuality, Ekklesia associate Savitri Hensman prepared a paper on 'Learning, Listening, Scripture and Sexuality'. This is a lightly edited version of that paper, submitted on behalf of the Lesbian and gay Christian Movement. Thanks to both Savi and LGCM (http://www.lgcm.org. uk/) for permission to reproduce it in this book.

2. P. Varnell, WWJD: Jesus on Anti-gay Slurs, http://www. independentgayforum.org/news/show/27000.html

Chapter Twelve

Will Rowan Williams rescue us from idiocy?

Simon Barrow

Sometimes, it must be admitted, journalism is the only thing that stands between the studiously-minded and their endless deferral of opinion. Equally often, however – and perhaps more determinatively in our impatient communications culture – journalism can betray the nuance and care of painstaking thought. At great cost to truthfulness.

Take the case of Archbishop of Canterbury Dr Rowan Williams' interview with Wim Houtman, religion editor of Nederlands Dagblad. After it first appeared on 19 August 2006, the Anglican leader's further remarks on the 'gay row' became yet more argued-over ballast in a vitriolic rhetorical war between those who wish for the full inclusion of lesbian and gay persons in the church, and those who would view that as a betrayal of the church's scriptural and traditional teaching.

At the time most seemed to agree on one thing, however. They thought that this interview indicated a significant shift in Dr Williams' position – away from his previous personal conviction that a change in the church's inherited stance against homosexuality would be theologically and pastorally appropriate. Quite clearly, however, it did not. What the Archbishop actually said is what he has been saying for a number of years: "I have to guard the faith and teaching of the Church. My personal ideas and questions have to take second place." This may be questionable, but it is not new.

He remarked that his now-famous lecture 'The Body's Grace', given at an event organised by the Lesbian and Gay Christian Movement, was received warmly by a few and critically by many. And he had the humility to acknowledge that a number of criticisms of the text were appropriate. He is, after all, a person with the kind of intellectual temperament that is always inclined to revise, qualify and enter renewed caveats. But he specifically declined the opportunity to modify, change or develop his personal approach to the question at the heart of current ructions in the worldwide Anglican Communion, declaring instead: "What I am saying now is, let us talk this through."

Diversity, disagreement and grace

Much of the rest of the interview, now somewhat buried in history, but still significant, was concerned with how Christian people might learn to handle their differences better and in a way shaped by the loving, gracious and patient nature of the Gospel of Christ. He also noted that this will take some time, given current obstacles on all sides, the intractability of much extant opinion, and the political challenges inherent in matters of church relations and structure.

Dr Williams made a further pertinent point about 'inclusivity' which lead his interviewer to conclude (wrongly, if you read what the Archbishop actually said) that he was offering, in Houtman's words, "a rebuke [to] those who argue it is high time the Church accepted gay relationships." Actually his comment – if it is to be read as a rebuke of any kind – was surely an invitation to all involved in the present argument to reconsider their attitudes to others.

What he said is: "I don't believe inclusion is a value in itself... Welcome is. [When] we welcome people into the Church, we say: 'You can come in, and that decision will change you.' We don't say: 'Come in and we ask no questions.' I do believe conversion means conversion of habits, behaviours, ideas, emotions. The boundaries are determined by what it means to be loyal to Jesus Christ. That means to display in all things the mind of Christ. Paul is always saying this in his letters: Ethics is not a matter of a set of abstract rules, it is a matter of living the mind of Christ."

Dr Williams continued: "That applies to sexual ethics; that is why fidelity is important in marriage. You reflect the loyalty of God in Christ. It also concerns the international arena. Christians will always have reconciliation as a priority and refuse to retaliate. By no means is everything negotiable for me". He then goes on to cite the Christian doctrine of the incarnation of God in Christ as an example of something "[constitutive] of what the Church is."

What is truly significant here, many would argue, is that the Archbishop did not say that our views on sexuality are a fundament of Christian community, rather that the person and work of Christ is. It is Christ who welcomes all, and bids them be converted to a fulfilled way of living based on reconciliation, faithfulness, non-retaliation and the sharing of life. Moreover, as Paul reminds us, it is not the case that some are pure and others impure as a whole, but that as we become part of the Body of Christ, broken and glorified, we each receive the opportunity to be reformed, both personally and corporately, from that which wounds and kills us and others.

This is the Gospel, and it applies to people of whatever condition and background, though it will impact them differently. As the relationships Jesus forges in the Gospels make clear, for example: the dispossessed will find dignity, the sorrowful will be comforted, and those who have arrogated themselves through wealth or status will discover that the company of Christ liberates them through sharing and humility.

Beyond 'inclusivity'?

The insufficiency of the language of 'inclusivity' (which we are then required to be for or against) is that it may blur this edge, suggests the Archbishop. As a signatory and supporter of the Inclusive Church statement (http://www.inclusivechurch2.net/), I still think he is right. I argued at the time that another epithet might have been chosen. Jesus, to be sure, opposes all the ways human beings (especially religious ones) try to exclude people from his company, touching the supposedly 'impure' and dining with those of ill-repute. The community (ekklesia) that he creates on the basis of God's uncontainable love is therefore graciously demanding in character. And this means that if we are to be one with it we will need to learn tough habits and counter-cultural skills: like enemy-loving, for example.

From my perspective (and from that of Rowan Williams' personal statements before he became Archbishop, I would suggest), these implications of Jesus 'love command' apply to all, whatever their gender, race, nationality, ability... or sexuality. This means that the Church needs to exclude, not whole groups of people, but behaviours such as violence, hatred, contempt, infidelity and abuse. And there is nothing in his Nederlands Dagblad interview – or in his wider writings and statements since – which suggests that Rowan Williams now thinks otherwise.

I would add another question about 'inclusivity' (as distinct from welcome) as the dominant Christian virtue for our times. And that stems from a meeting I once attended about the problem of homelessness. There church leaders and others were making extravagant statements about the need to 'include' everyone in the community. Until a single homeless person got up and said: "While I appreciate your desire to include me, can I just ask two questions? First, what will make this home you are offering better than the companionship I find on the streets? And second, will I be included in what you are building, or have you already decided that for me?'

Ouch. I took the point to heart, and have been concerned about the theological and practical weakness of the doctrine of 'social inclusion' ever since. What we need more than this is shared justice rooted in expanding love.

This takes us to another major challenge Dr Williams is issuing to all in the Christian community. We are too willing to couch our concerns in terms which fall short of what the Gospel offers and requires. If that is so of 'inclusivity' (which doesn't signal the kind of thoroughgoing transformation needed to make our personal and corporate lives really fulfilling) it is also true, the Archbishop says elsewhere, of the language of 'rights'. This is because, while rights speak of obligations towards each other which need to be enforced by law, the Gospel goes a step further and speaks of gifts which derive not from our human attempts to accommodate one another but from the unfathomable (and un-manipulatable) depths of the divine.

It follows, therefore, that if lesbian, gay, bisexual and transgendered people are to be welcomed alongside others into the Body of Christ (as I believe they most definitely should be), it should not finally be out of duty imposed by legal obligation, but out of love which recognises that the Church is incomplete without them (us) and what they (we) bring. Similarly, all who are freely baptised into the Church will recognise that their human fulfilment comes from One whose sacrificial love can re-unite us beyond compulsion, not from an uncritical inclusion which leaves unchanged that in each of us which divides and destroys. This might include chunks of 'queer' or 'straight' lifestyles.

Faithfulness not tribalism

What Dr Williams seems to be saying, therefore, is that self-styled 'liberals' often forget the transformational core of the Gospel and substitute for it a message of rights and inclusivity which underplays the Gospel's further gift and impact. And that what self-styled 'conservatives' often forget is that Jesus' toughest opponents often deemed 'scripturally faithful' certain ideas of purity and rightness which turned out to be human barriers against those who God especially loves – people deemed unacceptable within the established social order.

If this is so, then there is more in the Anglican Communion's 'gay row' than many activists on both sides are currently able to acknowledge. What is at stake is not a simple matter of rights or a simple matter of scriptural fidelity (both of which are deeply contested), it is the integrity (and out of that the unity) of the Christian Church as a subversive, levelling and creative community within the world.

"I just know that I have been given the task to preserve what unity and integrity there is", Dr Williams told Nederlands Dagblad. He may, as his many critics aver, have thereby underestimated the ploys of the warring parties, or the distinction between unity and conformity. He may be holding out for more than polity can deliver. He may be subjecting his own perspective too readily to inherited understanding. He may also be elevating unrealizable principle over the actual pain and injustice faced by lesbian and gay people – a very serious charge indeed. All this may be the case, and may weaken his position.

But if that is so, it is because the Archbishop of Canterbury also believes passionately and rightly that there can be no communion without transformation, no acceptance without faithfulness, and no beneficial change which does not involve the long, hard task of patient listening – rather than the self-righteous 'rush to judgment' frequently required by our modern media and governing cultures. Christ-likeness, in other words.

To put it another way, Rowan Williams is resisting all those who wish to collapse a difficult-but-life giving *mystique* into a convenient-but-deadly *politique* (Charles Peguy). So whatever we think of his proposed ways forward – I have a range of questions about what is currently on the table myself – we should welcome the fact that they are based on three important things. First, a deeply prayerful (de-centred) and theological (God-centred) mindfulness. Second, a willingness to talk and to listen widely, even as many within the 'debate' refuse to do so. And third, a vision of communion (rather than contract, chaos or conflict) as the only sufficient basis of transformational community.

These are subtle and demanding starting points. They have problems and challenges about them which, unlike many of his critics, the Archbishop is willing to debate and consider. But we should never overlook the fact that they concern a possibility of change which goes well beyond the insistent demand for 'victory' on each side (even mine!) and resides instead in an invitation to a Love much deeper than a flawed 'Hegelian dialectic' (Giles Fraser) and nothing like the 'spinelessness' (Gay and Lesbian Humanist Association) that some detect in his gentle words.

Staying thoughtful in an idiocratic age

Which leads to one last, important, area of questioning. Why is Rowan Williams' approach to Anglican divisions so readily misunderstood and mocked across the spectrum? Why are his consistent attempts to reframe our arguing regarded as so obscure or infuriating? When he was appointed as 104th Archbishop of Canterbury, few had a harsh word about him. Now he is frequently characterised as bumbling, weak and ineffectual.

This, I suggest, happens for two main reasons. First, Dr Williams has a vision of the church as an exemplary and life-expanding company of Godward people which many both within and without the institution have lost sight of or hope in. Second, he chooses his words with great care and nuance in a media culture which is ill-adapted to see either as a virtue, and in the midst of a dispute where complexity and ambiguity rapidly become political irritants. We do not want to hear what Rowan is saying, because it does not fit the mould of 'power leadership', and because we just want him to say what we are saying. If he doesn't, we are quick to accuse him of naiveté or betrayal.

This angry impatience with painstaking thought worries me. It is an early symptom, I believe, of the developing social condition identified and lampooned in an American movie called (without any attempt at pulling its punches) 'Idiocracy'.

'Idiocracy' is about a future where we have grown obese and lazy on consumption, immediate gratification and easy solutions. It portrays a culture in which loud-mouthed people with guns resent and despise disarmed, caring intelligence. They throw clumsy punches at the articulate and call them (ironically) "fags" for disturbing the know-nothing and change-less equilibrium.

Of course this is satire, far too black-or-white. And we are not quite there yet. Similarly, we need to recognise that in the Gospel's topsy-turvy world it is the good-hearted (not the self-selecting 'wise') who are blessed. Nonetheless, if we too readily dismiss the attempts of humane, spiritual and thoughtful people like Rowan Williams to point out that our difficulties are not just about someone else's blockheadedness, we may be nearer the idiocratic realm and further from the hoped-for realm of God and of reason than we think.

Especially if we haven't yet quite figured out what he is really saying because we are frankly too busy shouting and judging. As Jesus said to us all (not just 'that other lot'): "Let those who have ears hear."

Notes

1. This article first appeared as a feature ('How Rowan Williams can rescue us from Idiocracy') on Ekklesia in September 2006, and was modified slightly in May 2008.

2. Wim Houtman's interview with Dr Williams, rather unhelpfully entitled 'The church is not inclusive', is available in English on the website of Nederlands Dagblad.

http://www.nd.nl/htm/dossier/seksualiteit/artikelen/060819eb.htm

3. Information about the film 'Idiocracy' (script and screenplay by Mike Judge, 2006) is available at the Internet Movie Database - http://www.imdb.com/title/tt0387808/

Part Five: Changing

Chapter Thirteen

God Who Meets Us In The Flesh

David Wood

Part of the struggle going on within the church at the moment, about sexuality and much else, seems to me to be rooted in a fear of the flesh – embodied human living. Yet the Gospel celebrates the truth that God's proper name is Emmanuel, which means 'God is with us'. It celebrates the truth that God is one of us, the truth that God is within each one of us. God is all around us, rubbing shoulders with us in the street, looking back at us from strangers as well as friends. And the sign of this truth, of this reality, is desperately ordinary, entirely unexceptional. It is the Word made flesh – ordinary human flesh, not stone or ink or dazzling sky-works.

Every Christmas, therefore, we tell the story of how the maiden is with child and will give birth to a son. In other words, we get no blinding signal from heaven. The only indication we have to go on is totally natural, totally earthly; totally it seems from this human side of things. There is nothing special about it at all. It happens, as you might say, off-stage rather than centre-stage. And like every other sign it requires interpretation, for an uninterpreted sign points nowhere; an uninterpreted sign says nothing.

This means the reality of God is fragile indeed, fragile as a beautiful mist which evaporates as soon as the sun comes up, fragile as a new-born baby. It means God's power is unlike any power we know: powerful enough, confident enough, to be vulnerable, to be vulnerable to us, woundable by us. It means God values us, respects us, dignifies us, likes us, and loves us. It means God risks all, trusting us to recognise where love is being born and how we might hinder or help.

For God, you see, is not located in splendid isolation and security somewhere just beyond the farthest star. God is the next-door neighbour who is just a bit strange, just a bit different to us, who speaks broken English and seems somewhat threatening, but longs for our friendship. God is not Raphael's beautiful Madonna and

Child, frozen in time, enthroned serenely on our Christmas cards. God is the ragged Madonna and Child in the refugee boat, those desperate 'queue jumpers' turned back by an indifferent society.

God is not above our squabbles and confusions and violence, conveniently untouched and untouchable, immune from human suffering, immune to human joy. God is trampled underfoot as hard-won civil liberties are blithely whittled away in an age of terror, in this time of fear. God is crucified afresh in all our victims, crucified in every outcast, in every suspect and reject we toss on the scrap-heap.

I remember seeing pictures of some huge banners. I guess they must have been about a metre and a half wide and five or six metres in length, and they successfully turned a pretty featureless sports stadium into a worship space. Each banner appeared to be a random collage of faces - young and old, women and men and children, white and coloured, some smiling, some in pain, some hopeful, some despairing, some straight, some gay, some overfed, others dying of starvation.

The same four words were written across the foot of each banner: 'THE FACE OF GOD'. Here is what it means to be created in the divine image and likeness. This is what is meant when we claim that all human beings are icons of God, Christ's body in the world whether they know it or not. When God looks at me through your eyes I can be myself as I really am, without apology, without fear. When I see you as God sees you, sees you for the unique and sacred individual you are, you are freed to be real and true, relaxed and content

Being formed as a new people

Yes, we have been given a sign, a sign of who God is and where God is, and this sign contradicts everything we might expect. So the work of interpretation begins, and not just on Sunday (or at Christmas) but every day. From all eternity God's name is Emmanuel, from all eternity God is right here with us, yet God is always on the move. Seeking and serving this elusive God is not exactly rocket science, but there is nothing blindingly obvious about it either: it takes intelligence and sensitivity and a sense of humour. Above all, however, it is a journey of the heart. Indeed, it is a journey of the heart to the heart.

But how does this change of heart we need so badly actually happen? The Gospel of the Cross tells us that fullness of life can come only through self-giving, only through self-sacrifice. Yet none of this takes place automatically or magically or casually. In the end we all must choose for ourselves what has already been done for us in baptism. In the end it is all a matter of degrees, a matter of personal intention, of freely chosen discipline – and it depends more than we can ever fathom on who we mix with, more than we can ever know on the company we keep.

Principally, of course, becoming Christ-like swings on keeping close to Christ himself, being part of his living body. This means coming constantly to his bread-body lying on the table as members of his breathing-body standing around the table. And this can be hard work because we have no say at all in who our sisters and brothers might be. The table of Christ demands that we grow up, and growing up means learning to live with those we find awkward and uncongenial as well as those we warm to naturally. It means living in a community where we don't always get our own way, where we have to compromise to accommodate the needs of others who can be very different to us. It means allowing our rough edges to be knocked off, painful as that is sometimes. It means recognising that we have more to learn from those who irritate us, from those who provoke us, than we do from those who never ruffle our feathers.

A couple of years ago there was a television programme first shown in Britain, then around the world, that was rated in the UK as one of the most successful-ever broadcasts about religion, judging not only from the viewing figures but from the extraordinary reaction it produced – and by no means only from those who think of themselves as Christian.

In this series, five men were shown spending a month at Worth Abbey. Often to their surprise, they found their lives being turned around, upside-down, and inside-out - and by practicing on a daily and habitual basis (as well as a reflective, thoughtful and prayerful one), 'institutional religion' of all things! You may have noted from this programme and its derivatives that Benedictines take a fourth vow in addition to the usual monastic vows of poverty, chastity and obedience. Critically, Benedictine monks and nuns promise stability as well. They commit to this monastery, this place, this community. In other words, they can't run away when the going gets tough. They can't run away from each other, they can't run away from God, and they can't run away from themselves.

St Benedict and his followers have something vital to teach us here. Maturity for all of us lies in committing to this time, to this place, to this community of Christ's people. At times, as we all know, this is amusing, even hilarious; and we need no reminding that it can also be tedious and tiresome, even positively excruciating. Yet what is really achieved by taking our bat and ball and going home? Do we ever learn how to resolve problems that way? What do we ever learn about forgiveness and reconciliation if we keep taking the easy way out? Don't we just carry our pathologies with us undisturbed from one place to another, ready to stuff up again somewhere else? Only those who stay the distance know what the scaredy-cats never discover – that making-up is infinitely better than breaking-up. I am tempted to say, church 'splitters' please take note. But that would be just too self-righteous by half. If we are ever to mature, if we are ever to become adult lovers, women and men mirroring even small slivers of light and hope back and forth, bearers of faith and freedom instead of fear and slavery, we must go quietly and gently and patiently and prayerfully – each of us and all of us.

From judgement to grace

There is something fascinating about the second half of John the Evangelist's hymn to the Word made flesh. In John 1 29-42, Jesus walks through the narrative never speaking so much as a single word. John the Baptiser does all the talking, turning attention away from himself to the One who is more fully present than any other human being. 'Behold', he says, 'the Lamb of God.' He does not say as some English translations make him say, 'This' is the Lamb of God, but 'behold.' In fact, the Greek word simply means 'look.'

Behold, look - look for yourselves, see all that is to be seen, allow the eyes of your hearts free reign, take in who is really here. Look at the man Jesus of Nazareth and see someone sent from God, see God the Lamb who comes quietly, silently, in self-giving love. Behold the Christ who, by his sheer selflessness, by his total generosity of spirit, his absolute surrender to the Spirit's breath, prepares for us the way of freedom and peace.

John the Baptiser knows perfectly well that he cannot make his disciples see what he sees, that they are free to see or not to see, that no one can do this work for them, that each needs to catch the vision for themselves. Faith cannot be handed over or handed on like a game of pass the parcel. It is always a matter of opening eyes, always the hit and miss task of stirring imaginations, of evoking a sense of wonder, a sense of awe - not to conjure up what is not there, but to penetrate the veil, to touch the mystery. By all means let us be passionate about our faith; by all means let us be active in witnessing to its transforming power in all the places we live. But let us never get carried away, saying more than can be said, slipping over from zeal into zealotry, from belief into bigotry, from faith into fanaticism.

The Baptiser's disciples were around for a long time after his bloody death, faithful to their master, faithful to his vision of a steely-eyed God, a grim reaper meeting out justice left, right, and centre. Eventually, however, they disappeared – or so the historians tell us. But I wonder? I wonder if they didn't just become Christians of a particularly narrow stripe? For the puritans and the wowsers and the purity freaks are with us still. Indeed, they think they have the numbers and the money to take us over just at present, and there is no end to their bully-boy tactics because they passionately believe the end justifies the means. So hardly a day goes past when they are not throwing their weight around and shouting their heads off, impugning their opponents' integrity while pretending there is nothing personal about it – demonstrating by everything they say and do that they are indeed followers of John rather than Jesus.

Not – as I have already suggested - that I want to damn such people too quickly, for the point is that there is something of this harsh religion in all of us. It springs from our need to order our messy lives, to control our messy world. It arises in the murky depths of our own anxiety and fear. And Jesus' vision of God as the host of a marvellous party, a father who can't bring himself to throw his children out even when they spit in his eye, scares the living daylights out of us. The God and Father of our Lord Jesus Christ scares us to death because this God is no solution; this God is part of the problem. Yet this God, and this God alone, is the one who comes to us. This God alone, because in point of fact there is no other.

The Christmas story – actually, the Christian story - is that instead of John's pitch-forking judge we get a helpless baby. We get a wandering story-teller, a travelling healer, someone who brings out the best even in the worst of us, someone absolutely terrifying because he loves us even when we know there is nothing lovable about us at all. In the end, we get a man nailed up like a placard between two thieves, left to die in the sun - the wood of the cradle the wood of the cross cut from the same tree.

In truthful humility

Like it for not, here is God, the only true God, the merciful, the compassionate, who confounds all our expectations. Here is God who alone is worthy of worship and service, not some idol, our own day-dreams writ large, crafted according to our need and projected onto the heavens. 'Truly, I tell you, among those born of women no one has arisen greater than John the Baptist; yet the least in the kingdom of heaven is greater than he.'

And so back to the travails of the Anglican Communion, and many other churches at this time. Robert Runcie, one of the great 20th century Archbishops of Canterbury, liked to say there is a 'passionate coolness' about the Anglican way, but actually passionate coolness is characteristic of any faith worth the name. After all, every psychiatric ward has its share of people who are certain they are Jesus Christ, usually sectioned with those who are certain they are poached eggs.

Faith is not certainty. Real faith knows how little it knows and keeps us humble. It makes us more human, not less. And part of being truly human is to doubt, to sit lightly to what we hold most dear, keeping a sense of proportion, keeping a sense of humour, being wisely sceptical – especially about ourselves. We breathe a particular air, but sanity demands a window permanently open to catch different breezes. For however convinced we may be, however trusting of God, however sure of ourselves, it is always possible that we may be mistaken.

Note

These reflections are derived from traditional Advent and Christmas sermons preached in Grace Anglican Church Joondalup, in Perth, Western Australia.
See: http://www.joondalupanglican.com

Chapter Fourteen

Being consumed again by love

Simon Barrow

Reading the newspapers, listening to the radio, watching the television and pouring over the internet can be a sad experience when it comes to catching up with the churches and their seemingly constant arguing. How on earth can such wangling be brought to an end? What will give Christians a more realistic, humane and faithful grasp of what they should really be about? Where are the resources of transformation to be found?

The answer to these questions resides, many of us believe, in the neglected and transformative rites that already lie in our hands (quite literally). For each week, especially on a Sunday, Christians across the globe eat bread and wine together in anticipation of a new world coming – a world where sharing will be the norm rather than an exception or an "ethical option".

Communion, Eucharist, Mass. Call it what you will. To many outside the church (as well as a few within) it remains a bizarre and arcane ritual. But to those who view it as a key embodiment of Christian hope it is about being transformed by Christ into a Body bound together by inexhaustible love.

Insofar as this turns out to be true or false, everything else in the Christian life depends not just on "taking communion", but on the way that it is done – in the world, not just the sanctuary.

Consecrating bread at "the Lord's table" is an important act not least because it is, practically and historically, a profoundly dangerous one. For it calls into question who we are, who Jesus is, what bodies are, what sacrifice means, how God's peaceable kingdom comes, and what is truly involved in sharing – or not – the very stuff of life.

Since I am an Anglican who these days consorts willingly with Anabaptists, I also cannot afford to forget that some of my ancestors killed, and many of my wife's ancestors were killed, in disputes over what the bread of life really amounts to. And they did this,

Catholics and Protestants alike, without apparently realising that they were desecrating the very Body they sought to honour by their supposedly God-fearing actions. The warning to us about how we administer our tables could not be stronger.

Being liberated from destructive division

Yet the table of the Lord is still a place of conflict and division. In most cases, thankfully, Christians do not kill each other over doctrinal disagreements (like whether a piece of bread remains a piece of bread) today. But still, we as Christians deny each other in the presence of the Feast of Life. In my Anglican Communion, for instance (other churches can name their own examples) there are many senior bishops who will not share Communion bread with the Archbishop of Canterbury, because of a disagreement about whether certain people can be holy and acceptable before God.

The disagreement is theoretically about what we call today (in a way our New Testament forbears would not quite understand) human sexuality. But in fact it is also about who, if anyone, has the right to deny someone at Jesus' table.

Jesus himself was decisive about this. If you read the Gospels you will see that he caused a scandal by sharing bread and table fellowship with all who sought him – whether clean or unclean in the eyes of the law, acceptable or unacceptable to the religious authorities.

This wasn't an undemanding liberalism, however. To take his place at the table, the tax collector Zaccheus (in the famous story recorded in Luke 18. 10-14) needed to restore his relationship with those whose livelihoods he had robbed. Not because they wouldn't accept him (Jesus ate with him before his conversion), but because he needed to accept them as brothers and sisters. The blockage was in him. And eating with Jesus was its medicine.

God's realm is like this, says Jesus. It is a huge feast. And all are invited. The only issue is how we respond, whether we are prepared to be humble enough to share, whether we are willing to be changed forever by sitting at God's table as equals – rather than as rich and poor, Jew and non-Jew, male and female, gay and straight, taxed and taxing.

But at the moment of real crisis, his impending death at the hands of those who saw God's presence in him as the ultimate threat to their parochial power, Jesus did something even more shocking.

In talking to his friends, he spoke of his body as food, and he said that that as 'the Body', those who feed on Jesus, they (and we) are called upon to be consumed by, and consuming of, the divine love that becomes bread and flesh for us - is made available in the material. The immediate response was confusion (John 6.51-58). Is this man mad? How can a piece of bread be confused with flesh, and how can we possibly eat the flesh of Jesus?

According to St John, Jesus is exasperated. How can these people be so dumb? In speaking of himself as bread, Jesus is saying that the way, the life and the truth that he embodies (enfleshes) is the very substance of life – a kind of life that cannot perish and cannot be limited, because it is sustained by God not mere molecules. That is, the bread that Jesus is, that Jesus gives us and that Jesus invites us to be, is unlimited. It is a never-ending feast, and it cannot be the case that in consuming this bread we take food out of the mouths of others.

The bread of life is like the manna the wandering Hebrews found in the desert. There is enough for all and it goes on multiplying, so long as we do not try to restrict or hoard it. This is the way we are to live in a world where, as Tolstoy put it, "food for myself alone is a material issue; food for my neighbours is a spiritual issue." That is, bread is spiritual. That doesn't mean it is 'non-material', it means it is for sharing and developing life (which is precisely what the word 'spirit' means).

So when Jesus gives himself to us, inviting us to be one body with him (to consume him and to be consumed), it is life feeding on life, life generating life. This is the opposite of parasitism. The more we eat the more there is. The more there is the more we share. The more we share, the more people eat and the more there is to eat. And so on. This isn't 'religion' or 'superstition', it is a new way of living in the one world we all share. It is God's economy of plenty, and it works in almost the exact opposite way to conventional economics – because its currency is grace and friendship, not money and stock exchanges.

The feast of life – not death

However, the church that publicly claims Jesus, God's person, for its own, often operates in a quite different way. We feed not on Christ, but on each other, parasitically. We eat in an unhealthy way, seeking a monopoly on the Bread of Life - which is actually sheer gift. We seek to deny bread to others because they threaten us (by being "not like us" in certain ways). In so doing we betray the life-giving bread that Jesus is, and we demonstrate that we need to learn to eat anew. To "lay aside immaturity, simple-mindedness, and live, and walk in the way of insight", as the Book of Proverbs (9. 1-6) puts it.

In finding the table that truly is the Lord's (and therefore not ours, in any of our denominational guises) we will, says the Psalmist (34. 9-14), "depart from evil, and do good; seek peace, and pursue it." That is how we will know it is of God, and not merely a place of self-justification. But this is only possible if we are able to be transformed. And according to the Gospel we are transformed by becoming Christ's body, by being united with his flesh – which carries the ineradicable scars of crucifixion, but is also risen (glorified by the life-giving that is God's very self).

Being transformed, says Jesus, isn't a matter of being clever enough to think ourselves into the right state. It happens in a much more ordinary way when we eat bread together in his presence – as a matter of habit, rather than when we choose. It involves sharing bread with friends, and especially enemies. And it means seeking Christ's presence in the most unlikely, awkward, broken people – such as those we find immediately around us, perhaps!

This for me, as an Anglican, is what the whole ritual of Communion is about. Not mindless repetition, but an action through which the whole of the Gospel is made known, and I am located in God's story and united to others in Christ, continually and repeatedly. It is a way of "learning bodily" (not just in my head, where I spend too much of my time) – of practicing "Christly gestures" that become part of who I am when I am not at the table, as well as when I am.

The meal that transforms us

Of course, as those who know me best would be he first to tell you, this is a slow and painful process which sometimes shows the barest fruit. But that is why I need to be incorporated into a Body that does it with me and for me. I cannot do it on my own.

Let's just think about how this process works and how it re-tells the story of who we are.

We have bread and wine before us. We toiled for them, but they are still finally gifts. And we are thankful for them, for the life that God gives. We take the bread; we break it and share it. There is enough for all. No-one is outside the invitation to this feast, but there is a warning. If we truly share and eat we will be changed. As we eat the bread which is Christ, he becomes us. We become his body. So as we eat his body we eat ourselves – but not in a way that destroys, rather in a way that multiplies bread, flesh and hope.

It isn't magic. You don't need Aristotle's theories of essences and accidentals to understand what is going on. It is simply a way of saying that as we consume and are consumed by the love of Christ in each other, we nourish each other and are nourished. So is Christ present in this bread and this wine as we share them? That is the question that the church has often fought over in strange metaphysical ways which show us how easily we miss the point.

Of course Christ is present. But not in the bread and wine alone (the Roman Catholic Council of Trent called that idea "the sin of specificity", you may like to note). Christ is present in the whole event – in the people, in the sharing, in the words, in the gestures, in our hearts and in the new possibilities for the world that will flow naturally if we allow Christ's presence to change us. But Christ's presence is not just a comfort. It is a challenge. A test of our integrity. In our Anglican services we say these words: "We are one body, because we all share in one bread."

And the world shouts back, silently: "Hey, you Christians. Is that really true? Are you one body? Do you share the bread of life, or do some get loads of it while others starve? And not just at the Communion table, but in the real world, for Christ's sake! How goes the economy of Christians? Do they live as brothers and sisters who sit at table together? Does this breaking of bread mean anything, or are you kidding yourselves? The test is how you live. That is how we will know whether you are united with Christ, or just going through a little act." Perhaps this is why the Eastern Orthodox talk of service in the community as 'the Eucharist after the Eucharist'.

Being a community that truly shares bread

Let me end with a story which, for me, sums all this up. Some 24 years ago I was in Turin, in Italy, sharing Communion with a small group of Catholic Christians living on a run-down estate in the poorest part of town. They met weekly in an apartment to read the Bible and to reflect on their involvements in the work place and in social action. Always they shared bread and wine to remember Jesus' death at the hands of the powers-that-be, and to anticipate with celebration the solidarity of his risen life.

It was, in most respects, a standard Catholic Mass patterned on the Western Rite, though with prayers and words of their own, too. Significantly, the bread and the wine were blessed by everyone together, not a priest apart. There was also an urgency about it all. These people didn't need God's presence tomorrow, they needed it now.

Then something amazing happened. Right at the end, in Anglican and Catholic Communions, a priest will gather up the remaining bread and wine and consume it, to make sure nothing profane happens to it. It has always struck me as a little obscene that one person, representing the church as a whole, should gobble up the remaining Bread of Life while many in the world starve.

But, thankfully, that didn't happen in this community. Quietly, while we were still praying, olive bread and pizza, tomatoes and fruits, more wine and all kinds of other food began to appear on the Lord's table, which was at the same time a lunch table. And the bread and wine that had been our sacred meal suddenly became part of a huge Feast to which everyone was invited.

These Christians went ringing on the doorbells of all their neighbours with the good news. Free food, come and share! And if you want, bring some more to add to the feast. Needless to say, we were there all afternoon. And it was one of the most moving events of my life. The way they put it was that "life flows into the Eucharist and the Eucharist flows into life". And that's just how it felt. This is the kingdom. This is Communion. And it makes all the difference in the world.

So as Christians we gather to share the bread of life. And here is a humbling thought. However you understand that piece of wheat as it is pressed into your hands, there is a true sense in which what is happening is that Christ is voluntarily putting himself at your disposal. In the act of Communion, God, the alpha and omega, is choosing to be dependent upon us, deeply fallible human beings.

This may only be half the truth, but it is true nevertheless. And it dignifies us beyond belief. The question is, what we will do with Christ and the bread he gives us. Will we share it, will we hoard it, will we waste it or will we let it rise up in us to transformation? The decision, says God, is yours. But know that I will always go on giving life.

Note

This article, first published on Ekklesia on 8 August 2007, and revised in May 2008, was adapted from a sermon preached at Hyattsville Mennonite Church, Maryland, USA (http://www. hyattsvillemennonite.org/), on 22 July 2007.

Chapter Fifteen

Reconverting the Church

Jonathan Bartley

OK, so it's a bit of a cop out just to say that Christianity would be great if only it were practised properly - but I am far from the first to suggest it. G K Chesterton expressed it better when he proposed that Christianity had not been tried and found wanting... rather it had been wanted and never really tried.

Gandhi too, when asked once why he rejected the Christian religion said simply: 'Oh, I don't reject your Christ. I love your Christ. It's just that so many of you Christians are so unlike your Christ.'

Even the most cursory glance at the historical engagement of churches in public life shows that the love of enemies, forgiveness, hospitality, repentance, social equality and 'turning the other cheek' urged by Jesus has often been embarrassingly conspicuous by its absence.

That applies with equal force to the arguments Christians have been having among themselves, which often spill over into the public arena in ugly and disfiguring ways – as with the sexuality row, which as my colleague Simon Barrow points out, is as much about the struggle for security, identity and authority among wounded people as it is about the theological and biblical concerns in which it is often dressed.

But many do not trace the beginning of the incongruity between the message and its outworking to the foundation of the faith in Jesus and the movement of radical hope and change he initiated. Instead they suggest that the real conflict gathered force and pace toward the Fourth Century. Understanding what happened then can shed quite a bit of light on what's going on now.

It was the Roman Emperor Constantine who first brought Christianity to the heart of the empire. Identifying the cross as an instrument of conquest rather than healing, he gave the still fairly new faith a place within the official political and religious order.

In so doing, the Emperor confronted Christianity with an embarrassing dilemma which it could no longer avoid as settlement rather than sojourning beckoned.

Jesus or Constantine?

The early Christians had tended to take Jesus' words at face value. Many had refused to serve in the military, and believed in a form of equality and justice which was viewed as subversive to the social order.

The coercive and centralising interests of the state had little in common with the faith of Jesus. It was, after all, the oppressive institution that had colluded in putting their founder to death, and had subsequently unleashed waves of persecution against his followers.

An obvious way out of this problem was some sort of concordat, a way of saying 'look, if you give us status and security, we will offer quiescence and blessing in return'. It wasn't done for bad reasons, necessarily, but it failed to recognise the true costs – ones that would become all too apparent down the centuries.

But Christians now had to find ways of justifying their new position at the heart of empire. They had to explain their growing complicity in torture, imprisonment and war. They had to work out why their part in slavery and the death penalty was suddenly acceptable.

The result was some very nifty theological footwork which involved explaining away or sidelining Jesus' more difficult teachings and practices. Some did this by labelling them as naïve and impractical for the business of government. Others did it by devising theories which absolved the state partner from too much compliance with the way of God, or by spiritualising the Gospel (in spite of its central logic of the Word made flesh), or by separating the salvation (wholeness) of the individual from the salvation of the community.

A substantial public-private split began to take shape, in which Jesus' ethics were relegated to the private realm of personal relationships, or another world after death. A different form of Christianity, it was argued, was required for public life. This was one which began to copy the power structures and institutions of the world it absorbed itself too, and to reproduce them in the organisational, liturgical and priestly life of its own community.

The rest, as they say, is history. It would be wrong and simplistic to blame Constantine for everything bad that has happened in the name of Christianity since then, or to suggest that positive things didn't happen under Christendom. They did – but often from the underside and the margins, where the biblical-prophetic God of Jesus continually promises (and threatens) to be found, while 'the religious' and the political order looks elsewhere.

In this way, in 'diverse ways and places', the alternative dynamic of the reign of God – a kin-dom of love, rather than a kingdom of power – has continued to manifest itself, both inside and outside the organisations that have claimed to be harbingers of the Spirit's work.

Overall, however, the deal that brought us 'organised religion' in place of the subversive movement of Jesus, what many label 'Christendom', has blurred the meaning and impact of the Gospel for millions of people.

Beyond the 'church of power'

Now, 1700 years later, it is the Christianity of Christendom, rather than that which preceded it or looks beyond it, that seems ill-suited to public life and to the way the churches are trying to deal with their own struggles, their own future, their own organisation and the mission to which they are called.

Slowly it is dawning on many in the churches, as well as friends and foes outside, that Christianity is faced with a choice. It can hold onto its outdated power-ploys and be pushed out of public life completely (as hard-line secularists and the 'new atheists' want) – or it can think once again, as it did in the Fourth Century, about how it relates to the world around it.

The latter option is more likely, partly for reasons of expediency which have governed its approaches in the past. Things cannot go on as now if the church is to 'survive', as the negative typology puts it.

But there is no automatic path from privilege and power to witness and hope. Many will seek to cling on to vestiges or re-inventions of the Christendom settlements that have been unravelling so significantly in once 'Christian' Europe. They may even find allies from different parts of the world who are tempted to mistake the way of God (which is actually the way of self-sacrificial love) for a way of domination and self-assertion.

Much more hopefully, however, there are thousands upon thousands of followers of Jesus across the world who are hungering and thirsting for something different. They are fed up with a church of power and exclusion claiming to speak for them and to hold privileged access to the Gospel.

In all denominations and none, radical Christians (and those who want to follow Jesus, but find 'Christianity' so problematic) are searching for a fresh path; one which turns out to be the difficult road of discipleship trod by hosts of witnesses in the past – the 'new-ancient' way of the prophetic, biblical tradition, as theologian Walter Wink has put it.

Many within the historic peace churches (Mennonites, Brethren and Quakers), among base-level Catholic communities, progressive Evangelicals, Anabaptists, inclusive Anglicans, non-conformists, 'Jesus radicals', 'Christian anarchists' and others are making their voices heard and investing in new ways of being church, being witnesses, being politically engaged, being in conversation with others, being for justice and peace, and being God's people today.

Post-Christendom faith crosses all kinds of barriers that have been erected in the past as the church compromised its calling through ecclesiastical in-fighting and top-down politicking. The new movements for change are mostly not straightforwardly 'liberal' or 'conservative'. They are not 'modern', 'pre-modern' or 'post-modern' alone. They are neither backward-looking nor future-trendy.

Some in this new wave would call themselves 'subversively orthodox' – rooted in the historic Christian faith, but in ways that are generous but robust, provisional but purposeful, open but committed. They are oriented towards blessing rather than cursing, changing rather than chastising, engaging with the world rather than becoming 'victims' of a culture that no longer privileges Christianity.

In this sense, the church that tries to pattern itself on Jesus in the twenty-first century is what it has always been – a continuing, vulnerable, multi-faceted, odd community of people, visible and invisible, searching for the way beyond death and towards a different quality of life that is made possible by the gentle, disturbing power of the Spirit.

For the Gospel is about freedom not fear, and it calls a warring church to change – into a peacemaking one. To be converted, in other words. To receive a new heart that will show itself in deeds of justice and mercy.

There's a long way to go. But the place to start is here, and you are not alone.

Note

This article began life as one of a short series for the New Statesman magazine's website and was reproduced on Ekklesia as 'Why Christianity remains a novel idea'. It was expanded here in collaboration with my colleague Simon Barrow.

Notes on the Contributors

Simon Barrow *is co-director of Ekklesia. A commentator, theologian, consultant, journalist and educator, he was formerly global mission secretary and assistant general secretary of Churches Together in Britain and Ireland, the ecumenical body. His next book is* Threatened with Resurrection: The Difficult Peace of Christ *(DLT, 2008).*

Jonathan Bartley *is founder and co-director of Ekklesia, a think tank that looks at religion and public life, explores post-Christendom, and promotes transformative theological ideas. A writer, broadcaster and commentator, he has also taught political theology and authored a number of books, including* The Subversive Manifesto *(BRF).*

Glynn Cardy *is an archdeacon in the Anglican Church of Aotearoa / New Zealand and is vicar of St Matthew-in-the-City, Auckland. He went there in 2004 after many years as vicar of St Andrew's, Epsom, Surrey. He writes extensively about progressive Christianity.*

Deirdre Good *is Professor of New Testament, The General Theological Seminary (Episcopal Church), New York City. A widely published author, she is also a TV programme consultant on religious history. Her books include* Jesus' Family Values, *and* Mariam, the Magdalen, and the Mother, *essays on the Mary figures of the Bible. Thames and Hudson will publish her latest,* The Story of the Bible.

Savitri Hensman *was born in Sri Lanka and lives in East London. She is an Ekklesia associate and works professionally in the voluntary sector in community care and equalities. She is a respected and widely published writer and commentator on Christianity and social justice.*

Tim Nafziger *has been active with Christian Peacemaker Teams in the UK, USA and Colombia. He now works for CPT as outreach coordinator, builds web sites, and writes both for The Mennonite magazine's blog and for Young Anabaptist Radicals.*

He is an Ekklesia consultant and an evangelical Anabaptist.

Christopher Rowland *is the Dean Ireland Professor of*

the Exegesis of Holy Scripture at the University of Oxford. His interests include New Testament interpretation, apocalyptic in ancient Judaism and Christianity and the biblical hermeneutics of William Blake. He has published many books, including The Bible for Sinners.

Desmond Tutu *is a Nobel Peace Laureate and Archbishop Emeritus in the Anglican Church of Southern Africa. He is a well-known and outspoken Christian advocate for human rights and social justice.*

David Wood *is parish priest of Grace Church Joondalup and Anglican Chaplain to Edith Cowan University, Perth, Western Australia. He is author of* Poet, Priest and Prophet *(CTBI), a biography of Bishop John V. Taylor, one of the most widely acclaimed ecumenical mission theologians of the twentieth century.*

Further reading

This short bibliography includes works by the authors of this volume; references made by them; and a number of books on Anglicanism, Christian discipleship and allied concerns. Many of these books are available through Ekklesia's online partner The Metanoia Bookservice, located at the London Mennonite Centre. See: http://books.ekklesia.co.uk/

Andrew Bradstock & Christopher Rowland, *Radical Christian Writings: A Reader* (Blackwell, Oxford, 2002).

Simon Barrow (ed.), *Christian Mission in Western Society: precedents, perspectives, prospects* (Churches Together in Britain and Ireland, London, 2001).

Simon Barrow (ed.), *Expanding Horizons: Learning to be the church in the world* (Southwark Diocese, London, 1995).

Simon Barrow & Jonathan Bartley, *Consuming Passion: Why the killing of Jesus really matters* (Darton, Longman and Todd, London, 2005).

Stephen Bates, *A Church at War: Anglicans and homosexuality* (Hodder & Stoughton, 2005).

Jonathan Bartley, *Faith and Politics After Christendom: The church as a movement for anarchy* (Paternoster Press, 2006).

Jonathan Bartley, *The Subversive Manifesto: Lifting the lid on God's politics* (BRF, London, 2003).

Dietrich Bonhoeffer, 'The Theology of Crisis and its Attitude Toward Philosophy and Science', *Dietrich Bonhoeffer Works, 1930-31*, volume 10.

Helder Camara, *A Thousand Reasons for Living* (Darton, Longman and Todd, 1981).

Giles Fraser, *Christianity with Attitude* (Canterbury Press, Canterbury, 2007).

John Driver, *Images of the Church in Mission* (Herald Press, 1997).

Deirdre J. Good, *The Story of the Bible* (Thames & Hudson, forthcoming).

Deirdre J. Good, *Jesus' Family Values* (Church Publishing Inc., New York, NY, USA, 2007).

Deirdre J. Good, *Jesus the Meek King* (Trinity Press International, 1999).

Savitri Hensman, 'Re-writing History: the Episcopal Church struggle',
an Ekklesia/LGCM report -
http://www.ekklesia.co.uk/research/rewriting_history (19 July 2007)

Richard A. Horsley, *Jesus and Empire: The kingdom of God and the
new world disorder* (Fortress Press, 2003).

Nicholas Lash, *Holiness Speech and Silence: The question of God today*
(Asgate, 2005) – includes the 2002 Prideaux Lecture on 'Cacophany
and Conversation', given at the University of Exeter.

Kenneth Leech, *Subversive Orthodoxy: Traditional faith and radical
commitment* (Anglican Book Centre, Canada, 2002).

Kenneth Leech (ed.), *Setting the Church of England Free: The case for
disestablishment* (Jubilee Group, London, 2002) – essays, including
ones by Simon Barrow, Tom Hurcombe and Christopher Rowland.

Brian McLaren, *A Generous Orthodoxy* (Zondervan, 2004).

Stuart Murray, *Church After Christendom* (Paternoster Press, 2005).

Stuart Murray, *Post-Christendom: Church and mission in a strange new
world* (Paternoster Press, 2004).

Edward Norman, *Anglican Difficulties: A new syllabus of errors*
(Morehouse, 2004)

Michael Ramsey, *The Gospel and the Catholic Church* (Longman,
1963).

Jonathan Roberts & Christopher Rowland, *The Bible for Sinners:
Interpretation in the Present Time* (SPCK, London, 2008).

Christopher Rowland, *Christian Origins: The Setting and Character of
the Most Important Messianic Sect of Judaism* (Blackwell, Oxford,
second edition, 2002).

William L. Sachs, *The Transformation of Anglicanism: From State
Church to Global Community* (Cambridge University Press, 1993).

Desmond Tutu, *God has a Dream: A vision of hope for our time*
(Doubleday, 2004).

Simone Weil, *Gravity and Grace* (Bison Books, 1997).

Rowan Williams, *The Body's Grace* (LGCM, 1989 and 2002) – see
also: http://www.igreens.org.uk/bodys_grace.htm

Rowan Williams, *Anglican Identities* (Darton Longman and Todd,
London, 2004).

David Wood, *Poet, Priest and Prophet: Bishop John V. Taylor* (CTBI,
London, 2002).

John Howard Yoder, *The Politics of Jesus: Vicit Agnus Noster*
(Eerdmans, 1994).

Online resources:

Anabaptist Network UK:
    http://www.anabaptistnetwork.com/
Accepting Evangelicals:
    http://www.acceptingevangelicals.org/
An Anglican bibliography:
    http://gethsemanemarion.com/Bibliography.html
Anglicans Online:
    http://anglicansonline.org/ , also:
    http://en.wikipedia.org/wiki/Anglican
Annotated bibliography of resources on human sexuality -
    http://www.toronto.anglican.ca/index.asp?navid=367
Archbishop Rowan Williams:
    http://www.archbishopofcanterbury.org/71
Bridge Builders (London Mennonite Centre):
    http://www.menno.org.uk/bridgebuilders
Changing Attitude:
    http://www.changingattitude.org.uk
Ekklesia:
    http://www.ekklesia.co.uk
Episcopal Café:
    http://www.episcopalcafe.com/
Emerging Church Info:
    http://emergingchurch.info/
Faith in Society (Simon Barrow):
    http://faithinsociety.blogspot.com
Fulcrum: renewing the evangelical centre:
    http://www.fulcrum-anglican.org.uk/
Global South Anglican:
    http://www.globalsouthanglican.org/
Deirdre Good:
    http://notbeingasausage.blogspot.com/
Inclusive Church:
    http://www.inclusivechurch2.net/
Lambeth Conference:
    http://www.lambethconference.org/
LGCM:
    http://www.lgcm.org.uk/
On life, laughter and liturgy (Jane Stranz):
    http://stranzblog.blogspot.com/
Post-Christendom:
    http://www.postchristendom.com/
St Matthews-in-the-City, Auckland, NZ :
    http://www.stmatthews.org.nz/

About Ekklesia

http://ekklesia.co.uk/

Ekklesia is an independent, not-for-profit think-tank that examines the role of religion in public life and advocates transformative theological ideas and solutions.

A widely-referenced source of authoritative comment, policy ideas and news briefing on a range of contemporary issues related to religion and politics, Ekklesia has been listed among the UK's top 20 think tanks by The Independent newspaper. It has been profiled by the BBC, in London's Evening Standard and The Daily Telegraph, and has been described by The Times as 'influential'. Ekklesia now has one of the most widely read current affairs religious websites in Britain according to Alexa/Amazon rankings.

Ekklesia promotes post-Christendom approaches to social policy, nonviolence and conflict transformation, environmental action, the politics of forgiveness, economic sharing, support for migrants and displaced people, freedom of expression, restorative justice, a positive (relational) approach to sexuality, non-compulsion in religion and belief, the engagement of theology with science and culture, respectful engagement with those of other faith and non-religious convictions, and church as alternative community.

Ekklesia Book Service
(In association with Metanoia Books)

Ekklesia, the UK Christian think-tank that seeks to promote transformative theological ideas in public life, is pleased to run an online book service in association with Metanoia – the book store of the London Mennonite Centre.

For online purchases go to: http://books.ekklesia.co.uk/

We offer a book service with a unique collection of titles from both the UK and the USA, emphasising:

- mature theological thinking
- active Christian discipleship
- social justice and peacemaking
- conflict transformation
- 'emerging church' concerns

Metanoia is the British distributor of Herald Press (incorporating Faith and Life Press), the largest Mennonite publisher in the United States, and also imports titles from Pandora Press, Cascadia Publishing House and many others. We can obtain any North American title not normally available in the UK.

A particular specialism of the Ekklesia/Metanoia book service is Anabaptist studies, and titles relating to the developing debate about 'post-Christendom' in Europe.

Address
Metanoia / Ekklesia Book Service
14 Shepherds Hill
Highgate
London N6 5AQ

Telephone
Local Number: 0845 4500 214; International: +44 20 8340 8775
Fax: +44 20 8341 6807

Email: metanoia@menno.org.uk

Web: http://books.ekklesia.co.uk/

About Shoving Leopard

http://www.shovingleopard.com/

Shoving Leopard is a new, cutting edge imprint publishing works of spiritual and philosophical interest, with the aim of moving humanity on in its exploration of God and self.

Whether it be history, biography or fiction, we seek to expand our human level of understanding through reading.

Shoving Leopard seeks to attract those Christians who are under the radar; those slightly subversive thinkers really interested in Jesus but less interested perhaps in the rigid pale grey establishment view.

We take God's invitation seriously: 'Come, let us reason together'.

Letters to God from the Wilderness

Ronald Beasley

ISBN 1-905565-09-7
Paperback 220 pages
UK Price £12.95
US Price $20.00

Ronald Beasley was a Fellow of The British Association of Counselling & Psychotherapy, and practised as a Couples Counsellor/Therapist. He was an Elder and Reader of the Church of Scotland and initiated the Sea of Faith Group in Edinburgh. Ronald was a reluctant pacifist, yet with a clear commitment to non-violence. He delighted in music, poetry, and the Full Moon; valuing the zest of dialogue, good conversation, and quiet integrity.

Letters to God from the Wilderness is a deep expression of faith: the challenges, doubts and difficulties of a life lived in the close communion of an experienced counsellor with humanity. Ronald's questions are staging posts on his journey with God; issues with which we all wrestle, as Jacob wrestled with God in the desert. The book is a mature and honest appraisal of faith - a comforting and satisfying read, even where there are few answers.

Sadly Ronald Beasley was lost to us late in 2006. In his book, his spirit is so vibrant and his presence so tangible that we have decided to leave some of the text in the present tense. *Letters to God from the Wilderness* is dedicated to Ronald's wife Pam, and to members of his family.

Blackness & the Dreaming Soul

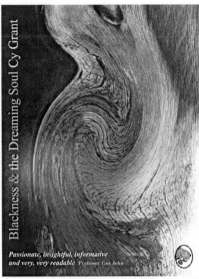

Cy Grant
ISBN 1-905565-08-9
Paperback
UK Price £14.95
US Price $25.00

Written without bitterness and recrimination, *Blackness & the Dreaming Soul* is neither pure biography nor philosophical manifesto, but grows out of the author's childhood as the great grandson of a slave in British Guiana. The book chronicles his career during a long sojourn in Britain, as a World War II RAF officer (two years spent as a prisoner of war in Nazi Germany), qualifying as a barrister at law, to a career in show business spanning stage, film, radio and TV. In the late 50s, Cy's was the first black face to appear regularly on television, singing the news in calypso.

In the 1970s, Cy Grant was chairman and co-founder of DRUM, the first black arts centre in Britain. In the 80s, he was Director of CONCORD multicultural Festivals, celebrating British cultural diversity when the idea of multiculturalism was not so popular. Cy is an Honorary Fellow of the University of Roehampton, a member of the Scientific & Medical Network and author of *Ring of Steel, pan sound & symbol*, the story of the evolution of the Trinidad Steelpan.

"Blackness & the Dreaming Soul" does not pull its punches - it has its finger smack on the pulse of what is eating away at the very heart of civil society in Britain.
Professor Gus John

Printed in the United Kingdom
by Lightning Source UK Ltd.
131488UK00002B/199-231/P